START WORRYING:

Details to Follow

START WORRYING:

Details to Follow

ALBERT VORSPAN

An Insider's Irreverent (But Loving)
View of American Jewish Life

UAHC PRESS • New York, New York

Library of Congress Cataloging-in-Publication Data
Vorspan, Albert.
    Start worrying : details to follow : an insider's irreverent (but
loving) view of American Jewish life / by Albert Vorspan.
      p.   cm.
   ISBN 0-8074-0462-4 : $7.95
    1. Jews—United States—Anecdotes. 2. Jewish wit and humor.
I. Title.
E184.J5V68 1991
973′.04924—dc20   91-22708
                                                  CIP

This book is printed on recycled paper ✪
Manufactured in the United States of America
10 9 8 7 6 5 4 3 2 1

To my wonderful wife, Shirley, who, having listened to my punch lines for over forty years, loves me nevertheless, and to our five (so far) grandchildren—our claim to immortality—who are great kids with sharp wits and these sunny names: Emily, Zachary, Ben, Sammy Ray, and Jonah.

ACKNOWLEDGMENTS

I want to express my appreciation to Dorothy Albelo and Esther Kornecki for their painstaking and patient skills in typing this manuscript; to Annette Abramson for her careful and caring copyediting; to my editor, Aron Hirt-Manheimer, for his superb judgment and editing; to Stuart Benick for transforming a manuscript into a handsome publication; and to David Saperstein and Dan Syme, colleagues, who encouraged me to undertake this volume.

ACKNOWLEDGMENTS

CONTENTS

PREFACE

For a shy and modest person like me, who has so much to be modest about, having a book on the best of my writings–published while I am still alive yet–is a hair-raising experience. And anyone who has seen me knows how badly I need a hair-raising experience. Four decades of talking off the top of my head has left me bald and beautiful.

This book is a major ego trip for me, obviously, but it is also somewhat embarrassing. Empires do not rise and fall on the nuances of my words. A few years ago I was introduced at one of our temples by an enthusiastic chairman who extolled me to the heavens in the following words: "Al Vorspan has made contributions to Jewish life—indeed to America—nay, to all humanity—that can only be described as—*infinitesimal.*"

Why does a guy who has served for thirty-eight years as director of social action for the Union of American Hebrew Congregations, the central body of Reform Judaism, write Jewish humor? Because Jews produce humor the way we produce shmaltz herring, stuffed derma, and Nobel Prize winners. Throughout Jewish history, Jews have learned, in an absurd world, to laugh in order not to cry.

Of all the factors contributing to Jewish survival—notably our religious tradition, our faith, our sense of family, our collective memory, our cultural inheritance—maybe the real survival kit has been the Jewish capacity to laugh at our troubles, at our bureaucracies, at our enemies, and even at ourselves. In one of my books, I explain these things and conclude: "Tell me, have you seen any Babylonians around lately?" One of my friends phoned me and said: "Hey, Vorspan, I read your book, and I loved that *shtick* about the Babylonians. Indeed," he raved on, "when I read that paragraph to my Yiddish-speaking mother-in-law she *kvell*ed. I said, 'Mommele, have you seen any Babylonians around lately?' She smiled and said, 'Listen, since I got old, I don't get out of the house much anymore. But you wouldn't have to tell me the neighborhood has changed. . . . If you treat them good, they'll treat you good!' " So there you have it.

Social concern, spiced with humor, is a tasty Jewish recipe. Indeed, in the world in which we live, obsession with the grim issues of our time makes humor indispensable to sanity. Who can cope with a Saddamized world of Arafats and Assads, Dukes and Farrakhans, and endless Jewish meetings without relief?

This book will tell you how to identify Jews, how to survive Jewish meetings and fund-raisers, how to name your kids and your kids' kids, what would happen if peace really came to Israel, what it will be like when we have our first Jewish president, and how to cope with many similarly crucial issues. Some of this material appeared in my book, *My Rabbi Doesn't Make House Calls* (which one reviewer mistakenly identified as "My Rabbi Doesn't Make Housewives"). This book decodes many of the anomalies of Jewish life. For example, Jews have never in all of history been as free, as prosperous, or as educated as we are in America. So how do we react? *Gevald!* Weren't Jews in pre-Hitler's Germany also free, prosperous, educated? *Nu?* In Spain we had a golden age yet, and what happened? They kicked us out, one, two, three. So do you think it couldn't happen here? You don't have to see anti-Semitism or feel its hot breath. It's there, germinating under the rocks, waiting for the right moment. Good times are the most dangerous because they lull you into false security. Many Jews assert that an occasional burst of anti-Semitism not only keeps the juices churning, but it keeps the Jews Jewish. And a sense of humor, looking at a crazy world through our own Jewish lens, helps to keep us sane and human.

This Jewish people has kept alive not only its sense of humor but also its sense that there is a Jewish mission to make the world a better place. The idea of *tikun olam*—repairing the broken world—is as ancient as this 4,000-year-old people and as fresh and urgent as this morning's headline. Jews have more reason to give in to despair and fatigue than perhaps most other peoples (don't start up with Kurds, Armenians, Cambodians, Palestinians), but, for the most part, we have had the staying power and the stamina to keep up the fight for a decent America and a peaceful world. That is our immortality: to believe, against all odds, that a Messianic Age is really possible. It will not come in my lifetime, of course. And, if it did, with my *mazel,* I would miss it. When my ship comes in, I will definitely be at the airport! *Life* magazine once ran a cataclysmic article about the impending disappearance of the Jewish people. *Look* magazine followed with a similar protentous obituary. *Life* disappeared, *Look* is gone, and this stiff-necked Jewish people still sits around in a hundred lands, asking questions about the puzzlement and meaning of Jewish existence and finding a hearty laugh about it all.

Over almost four decades of professional service in the Jewish world (forty years on Jewry duty), I have survived more meetings, eaten more egg salad and tuna fish sandwiches, stolen more good lines, and enjoyed more good laughs than anybody else I know. More would be illegal. The laughs I scribbled down and collected helped me endure the frustrations.

If this book is the embodiment of all this experience, all this wisdom, all this insight, and all these snippets of notes, why is it so slim? Small is beautiful.

1

How to Identify a Jew (Though He or She Doesn't Look Jewish)

It is hard to identify a Jew. In the first place, you don't have to be a Jew to be "Jewish." Some Jews are not "Jewish." The late Lenny Bruce, who was Jewish, considered Italians "Jewish." When Italians formed the Italian Anti-Defamation League, the Jewish Anti-Defamation League thought the Italians were getting too Jewish. When American Arabs also formed an Anti-Defamation League, the Jewish group exclaimed enough already and sued. The Irish that give up the Church are "Jewish," as are Ivy League Asians. So were blacks until they became Afro-Americans. So it's not easy to figure out who's Jewish.

Scientists have proven there is no such thing as a Jewish race. Religion doesn't define Jews because many Jews reject all religious belief. How can you figure a people that includes some parents who name their kids Joshua and Sarah and rear them to be atheists or Unitarians while other parents brand their young ones Lancelot and Toni and enroll them in Jewish day schools? So exactly what is the Jewish group? How do we define it? We can't agree on what we are, but at least we know what we are *not*. We are not WASP, but are we WASH (White Anglo-Saxon Hebrews)?

The most controversial issue in Jewish life is What is a Jew? A Jew has been identified as somebody who goes around asking "What is a Jew?" That controversy stands a better chance of blowing up the State of Israel than do the Arabs.

Nor is there such a thing as a Jewish physical type—no Jewish nose, hair, eyes, skin color, height, etc. For proof, one has only to go to Israel and survey the Nordic-looking, blue-eyed blond, snub-nosed young sabras (native-born Israelis), alongside the black Jews from Ethiopia. Who is Jewish? What is a Jew?

This Is a Jewish Neighborhood?

Some people think you can identify Jews by the neighbor-hoods they live in. Most Jews live in Jewish neighborhoods. But, even if we knew what a Jew is, what is a Jewish neighbor-hood? What percentage of the people are Jewish? Nobody knows. A typical Jewish neighborhood has a Chinese restau-rant named Sui Generous, a pizza parlor, a beauty shop, a kosher deli, and five synagogues—Reform, Conservative, Or-thodox, a split-off from one of the temples (usually called Temple Shalom, peace), and a split-off from the split-off. The great benefit from living in a Jewish neighborhood is that then you don't have to do anything Jewish. Nobody asks. It's an effortless Jewish life. In small towns, where Gentiles predomi-nate, Jews must belong to synagogues. Christian friends ask: "How come your Debby doesn't go to Sunday school?" and "Tell me, to what church do you go?" And the first thing you know, some nice people from the local Christian church raise some money for a site and are out on the lot with hammers and saws to start a fellowship project, building a "church for our Jewish neighbors." For a Jew to refuse to belong is heresy to the American religion of ecumania.

Sometimes, of course, a Christian neighborhood becomes a Jewish neighborhood. This happens when an influx of Jews results in an exodus of non-Jews. This pattern has been evident in many suburbs. Some Long Island communities became Jewish almost overnight in the post-World War II era. Some Jews moved in; non-Jews began to move eastward. Then some

Jews moved further east on Long Island; non-Jews ran faster. One demographer observed the phenomenon and asked: "When will the non-Jews stop running eastward?" The answer: "Past Montauk, when their hats begin to float."

But the cycle never stops. After the non-Jews flee from the Jews, and the neighborhood becomes Jewish, the first black families move in; the Jews begin to flee from the blacks, leapfrogging on the heels of the WASPS, who are fleeing from both of them, closely followed by the blacks who are now moving out of their neighborhood (the Puerto Ricans are coming) that was recently a Jewish neighborhood and just before that had been WASP and *Judenrein.* Where will it end? Perhaps with integrated hats floating at Montauk.

And yet, incredibly, Jews can usually identify each other. There is a strange subliminal alchemy of intuition, guesswork, and sensitivity that leads Jews to be able to locate the *landsman* (fellow Jew). How do they do it?

Locating the Landsman

LTL (Locating the *Landsman*) is a Jewish game played a hundred ways. In reading the newspaper, one's eye automatically flags Jewish-sounding names. If the paper is announcing the Nobel or Pulitzer Prize awards, some internal computer notes how many of the winners are Jewish. If thousands of scholarship winners are listed, the eye grows bleary, proudly picking out Jewish boys and girls who have earned honors en route to college. If, after an airplane crash, the paper lists the victims, there is of course a general shudder of horror shared by all readers. For the Jewish reader, there is an additional involuntary sigh for one's ill-fated coreligionists. If a scandal explodes on page one and the culprits are listed, in a subliminal and anxious flash, any Jewish names are recorded in the mind's eye of the Jewish reader. The brain may even trigger a grimace on the reader's face and bring an audible *oy* to the lips. Why? Perhaps because the Jewish group is so small, its history so tormented, and its sense of common destiny so acute.

LTL is also applied to entertainment—movies, television, literature, sports, theater. Through a magical intelligence system that flashes information faster than a satellite, Jews know that Jerry Lewis, Marv Albert, Milton Berle, Sandy Koufax, and Saul Bellow are members of the *mishpocheh* (family). Imperialistic Jews tend to be expansionist, stealing across the borders for new conquests. Thus they seek to claim Debbie Reynolds (she has been married twice to two nice Jewish boys—one at a time) and the late Danny Thomas ("if he wasn't Jewish, he should have been"). But this is cheating and, if challenged, calls for surrendering three *landsleit* you have already successfully located. So one must be careful before making a claim. To test your own LTL score, check which of the following you believe are or were Jewish:

Roseanne Barr	Bob Dylan
Howard Cosell	Theodore White
Ted Koppel	William Safire
Kitty Dukakis	Bob Simon
George Burns	Wolf Blitzer
Paul Newman	Beverly Sills
Irving Wallace	Walter Matthau
David Lee Roth	David Cone
Woody Allen	Gen. Norman Schwartzkopf
Geraldo Rivera	Pat Buchanan
Henry Kissinger	Donald Trump
Tom Okker	Jean Harris
Lorne Greene	Sam Donaldson
Robert Maxwell	Tom Wolf
Alan Arkin	Senator William Cohen
Whoopie Goldberg	William Simon
Simon and Garfunkel	Jerry Orbach
Paul Simon	

The answer is that all except the last ten are (or were) Jewish. Score four points for every correct answer. Ninety to 100 percent is excellent; 80 to 89 percent is good; 70 to 79 percent is embarrassing and means LTL is not your bag. If you scored less than 70 percent, are you Jewish? You don't look Jewish!

LTL can also be played backwards by going back into history. High points are given for such bona fide claims as: (a) Pope Anacletus II, in the years 1130-1138, was known as a "Jewish pope" (he was the grandson of a Jewish convert to Catholicism); (b) Columbus had a Jewish navigator named Judah Cresques (known as the "Map Jew"); (c) Luis de Torres, Columbus's interpreter on his first voyage, coined the word "turkey," calling the bird *tukki,* Hebrew for "peacock"; (d) behind George Washington was a Jewish financier, Haym Salomon, who called cards and helped make the American Revolution possible; (e) Judah Benjamin, who held such important positions as attorney general, secretary of state, and secretary of war in the Confederacy, was Jewish; (f) Jesus was a Jew (technically you get points for this, but it's not worth the hassle).

In playing LTL, one should be armed with as many of these historical tidbits as possible. You must give up four *landsleit* if you use the same tidbit twice. After all, one should not be a bore in playing LTL. In playing backwards, one must also be on guard not to claim a non-Jew as a *landsman.* Lately, overzealous Jews have claimed Columbus, the painter Rubens, Pope John, and Colin Powell (he speaks Yiddish, thinks British, and is Afro-American). If challenged, such a false claim will cost you ten hard-won *landsleit.*

Dropping the Landsman

The other side of the LTL coin is DTL (Dropping the *Landsman*). This game is essential because LTL always turns up a few Jews you don't want, and there must be a way of disposing of them. Who needs to claim Karl Marx, the progenitor of Communism; or Meyer Lansky, the reputed financial brains of the mob; or (remember you can play DTL backwards, too, just like LTL) the bloody Jewish King Herod (a Roman Quisling in the first century before the common era)? DTL is the way of disposing of unsavory characters like the above as well as chronic losers or *nudniks.*

Let's take Karl Marx, for example, to see just how DTL works. You are asked: "Say, was Karl Marx Jewish?" The answer: "No. He was born Jewish, but he was baptized in childhood, grew up as a Christian, and became an anti-Semite. Besides, he was the prophet of Communism, which has done about as much for the Jews as cholera!" That, of course, is a valid DTL (what with his conversion, etc.). You win three good *landsleit* for shucking such an obvious bad one.

Let us turn to a stickier case. A man named Matthew Goodman, a vice-president of the local bank, embezzles a half million dollars, runs away, and hides in Tunis. It is widely believed that he is Jewish, and the surface evidence seems to sustain the findings. You must approach this DTL in a gingerly manner: "Well now, let's just see. Matthew? Matthew? That's not a Jewish name, is it? Did you ever read the Christian Scriptures? Matthew was one of Christ's apostles, and his books are not exactly pro-Jewish, I'll tell you. Vice-president of the bank, eh? Are there any Jewish officers in that WASP bank? So why should they make that embezzler vice-president? What do you mean, that's not logical? Besides, if he were Jewish—the only Jewish officer in the bank—do you think he would disgrace his people that way? No, he would pause, with his hand in the till, and say: 'Will this be bad for the Jews?' And what is the answer to that question? Obvious! And then he flew away to Tunis? Now I ask you: 'What kind of a place is that for a Jewish fellow who has just become *ongestupped* (wealthy)?' If he were Jewish, he'd go to Argentina, nice Jewish community, good delicatessens, hot knishes, pickles, a little Yiddish culture, UJA, Israel Bonds, Jewish theater. Tunis—Arafat land? No, it doesn't figure. If he were really Jewish, he would go down to Mexico City, probably on an American Jewish Congress package tour. Did you ever see the Jewish Sports Club there? Tennis, swimming, volley ball, golf, dancing, a kosher snack bar—a real *mechayeh*. No way, José, this Goodman is no Jew. Are you kidding me?"

This DTL is definitely worth a pickup of two good *landsleit*. **Tip:** Disposing of Roseanne Barr and Robert Maxwell would earn you a bonus of five *landsleit* and lots of plaudits.

2

How to Organize, Avoid, and Survive Jewish Meetings

It's been said that a committee is a group of the unwilling, picked from the unfit, to do the unnecessary. For Jewish meetings, this is an understatement.

"Well," says the chairman, glancing at his watch, "it is now after eight-thirty (it is really ten to nine, but who's counting?), and the meeting was called for eight. In fairness to those of you who came on time and also to our out-of-town speaker (if it were a *local* speaker, we could fiddle around until after nine), I think we should get started."

The chairman balefully surveys the small audience scattered among row after row of empty seats (I told them they should set up the smaller room; this speaker is as popular as the German measles) and says: "I am sure that more people will be coming along. However, in looking over the audience (why do Jews never sit in the first two rows?), I want to assure the distinguished speaker that these people sitting in front of him came here despite the severe competition of other cultural events in town (television) and that we certainly have quality here tonight (quantity we don't have).

"And now, without further ado, I would like . . . (what I would like is to get the hell out of here by eleven at the latest, in time for 'Nightline')." The role of the chairman is to say nothing, and he does so admirably and at great length.

And so begins another Jewish meeting. Jewish meetings

have a ritual, a drama, and a flavor all their own. The constant nature of Jewish meetings is doubtless responsible for the low Jewish birthrate. From the moment the meeting begins (late) to the moment it ends (late), after a long hassle as to the time and place of the next meeting, it is a uniquely and wonderfully Jewish experience. The following are some of the basic rules for such meetings:

The Out-of-Town Speaker

Enthusiasm for the speaker is in direct proportion to the distance he had to travel. Don't make the fatal mistake of inviting Dr. Paul Bretman, a genuine authority who happens to live in your own community. The chairman would introduce him as "our own good friend and neighbor, Paul," and everybody would head for the exit. If he lives in Chicago, Paul is good south of St. Louis and east of Detroit. That is to say, if your speaker comes from a hundred or more miles away, he will qualify as "that distinguished expert." (The imagination boggles at the thousands of out-of-towners jetting in and out of each other's towns each night in a mammoth game of flying musical chairs.) Anyway, you will not invite him back again, which, since he is a hit-and-run speaker who has one speech and much prefers one-night stands, is fine with him, too. He's what's known on the circuit as a "Chinese-menu speaker": two jokes from A and three clichés from B.

The Introducer with Foot-in-Mouth Disease

Pick the introducer with care, either rewarding someone for a generous gift, setting him up for a future gift, or calming the *macher* (top gun) whose wife was insulted at the planning committee. The introducer should, under no circumstances, have the vaguest familiarity with the speaker and his background. It's obligatory that he scramble the letters of the speaker's name (Dr. Robert Druck should come out Rubber Duck and Rabbi Finstein as Rabbit Finster).

He will read every word of the biographical sheet, provided in advance by the speaker, so the audience will not be deprived of the knowledge of how the speaker skipped the fifth grade in the St. Louis public schools, how his was the first bar mitzvah ever celebrated in the Cow Palace in San Francisco, and how, during World War II, he developed a double hernia carrying cases of beer for sailors on Mog Mog Island in Ulithi in the Pacific. The last line of the introduction should reflect the introducer's own distinctive flourish. Here are three examples:

"I have been assured by those who have heard the speaker before that, when he finishes his address to us, we will be absolutely thrilled."

"Of all the ranking dignitaries who have adorned this platform, I believe that our speaker tonight is the rankest."

"All of us have heard a great deal about this man whom we are honored to have address us tonight, so the less said about the speaker the better."

Overprogram the Meeting

Start the meeting with an invocation. This not only pays proper respect to religion but permits the rabbi (who knows the out-of-town speaker very well and has the highest contempt for his ability) to give to *God* the speech the rabbi should have been invited to present to the *audience*. During the invocation, the members of the planning committee will recall how furious the rabbi had been when asked to pronounce the invocation. ("When will you people learn that a rabbi is something more than a mere invoker and benedictor?") They also know from previous experience how much angrier the rabbi would have been not having been asked.

After the out-of-town speaker has finished, it is good form to have a panel of five of your own members: a sisterhood lady, a youth, a man from the men's club, a representative of the "big board," and the group's house intellectual (who always says, "This was very *interesting* and *stimulating,* but I think we must ask ourselves several prior questions: Precisely what is our purpose, how do we define that purpose, and how do we propose to achieve that purpose?"). While it would be faster and equally useful to have the panel speak simultaneously, there is a higher value in repetition. Long before the panel is done, the audience will have succumbed (being speeched to death is the Jewish form of capital punishment), and the out-of-town speaker will be on a jet winging to Detroit (his plane passing two thousand feet under the plane speeding Paul back from Tulsa).

Watch the Logistics

The success or failure of the meeting depends largely on the facilities. If it is a banquet, every person should be seated at the four-tier dais so that nobody feels like a second-class citizen.

If, on the other hand, you want to have a conference-type meeting, with give-and-take discussion, have the tables set up either in a T (with the chairperson and other *macher*s crossing the T) or in a U (with the brass at the bottom). Some Jewish organizations have experimented with the double-wing and the I-formation. The double-wing has certain advantages (eat on one wing and meet on the other), but those on the end of the wing tend to fly out the door too easily. The I is excellent if you have cochairpersons for your club (one on each end of the I), but the people on the vertical line tend to exhaust themselves spinning their heads back and forth like the shuttlecock in a badminton game. The new procedure is a series of separate tables, which simplifies separate checks and also lends itself to buzz sessions, a technique of group dynamics by which small groups are able to evaluate the main address and pose such basic questions as: "When's lunch?" "Who found *that* speaker?" "What's *Jewish* about our Jewish organization?" "When's this thing over?"

Follow the Leader

There are subtle ways to stand out in a crowd, even at a meeting. If you watch closely, you can pick out the natural leader even if he never opens his mouth. He arrives late and breathless and shakes hands all around before settling into a seat next to the chairperson. ("Sorry I'm late—the earliest I've been late all year.") Later he will leave early with similar flourishes. In the midst of the proceedings, he will be summoned to a long-distance telephone call. ("Is Dr. Jerome Keeler in the room?")

More important, Dr. Keeler will be the very eye of a hurricane of note passing during the meeting. Although he will look completely intent on what the speaker is saying and seem to be taking copious notes on his remarks, he will actually be conducting a rapid-fire simultaneous exchange of notes with at least ten people at the table (one of whom is, of course, positioned at the very opposite end of the room).

A favorite postmeeting pastime is piecing together the fragments of notes left in the ashtrays. (Unshredded notes are not worth the bother.) Here are some excerpts: "Man, is this guy a bomb! He's been talking an hour, and he hasn't said anything yet." . . . "Boy, this Rosenblut is a lousy chairman. How did we ever get stuck with him? Do *you* want to be the next chairman? I can swing it!" . . . "Stop wasting paper!" . . . "Dear me, I am sending this note to myself, all the way around the table. I'm sick and tired of everybody getting notes except me. You don't have to answer this, but it puts me in the swim."

The Space Race

How do you know if your meeting has been successful? By the number of people who attend? No! The Grateful Dead can fill Yankee Stadium; what does it prove? By the amount of money raised? No! This is important, but it is not the best criterion. There is only one valid measure: space in the *New York Times* (or the biggest daily paper in your town). If it's not in the *Times,* it did not happen. If it earns a mere one or two paragraphs, it happened, but barely. If it gains a full column with a byline, it's carved in stone.

Conventional Wisdom

National Jewish conventions where thousands of delegates gather for an extended period (up to a week) at a big city hotel start a day early to give delegates time for hugging and kissing. Then the programing kicks in. Sessions begin with 8:00 A.M. continental breakfast meetings and continue through forums, workshops, committee meetings, fund-raising luncheons, plenaries, caucuses, receptions, banquets, and evening programs until 3:00 A.M., when the resolutions committee begins its work and continues until a quorum is ossified.

Only a few mammoth hotels throughout the country can accommodate the national conventions of the biggest Jewish organizations. Among these are the Fairmont in San Francisco and the Century Plaza in Los Angeles. These are favorite hotels for conventions whose themes are poverty and racial integration. Many delegates to a recent convention can still remember the swinging workshop on "Our God Commanded War on Hunger and Homelessness," which was held in the Boom Boom Room of the Fontainebleau. Delegates to this particular hotel now carry maps of the hotel pinned to their lapels; this is to make certain that there is not a recurrence of the regrettable lapse in which eighteen B'nai B'rith delegates got hopelessly lost trying to get from A Wing to F Wing and were baptized intravenously at a Southern Baptist workshop on "How Do We Reach Our Jewish Brethren?"

The Resolutionary War

One of the purposes of the convention is to legislate, that is, to make policy for the organization. This is done by the adoption of resolutions. Jewish life has not advanced much beyond the *resolutionary* phase. There are several vital rules for the preparation and adoption of resolutions. There are, of course, no rules for the *implementation* of these resolutions. (It is analogous to swatting flies. You don't have to do anything with the flies once you've swatted them. The fun is in the process.)

Here are some of the rules:

1. The resolutions should be written in advance by members of the staff. (How would *delegates* know which resolutions they need?)

2. They should be presented to a resolutions committee, which meets nonstop for three days and nights until the very moment the resolution is presented to the plenary session. In that way they will be too bleary to do any real damage.

3. The first paragraph of the resolution should quote from Isaiah, thus setting forth the Jewish rationale for the resolutions on second-class mailing privileges, air pollution, or the tax on Brazilian coffee. (Don't use "Come let us reason together"; it's been overdone.)

4. The second paragraph should cite "our commitment to those ideals that underlie both our faith and democracy itself," thus lining us up squarely with the free world.

5. The resolution should contain at least twelve whereases and two caveats, thus establishing that we're not shooting from the hip.

6. The last paragraph should constitute a peroration like "In this way we will advance man and society toward that Kingdom of God, which has been our goal and our vision since the Hebrew prophets first sounded the trumpet call of conscience to all mankind." (This will provide the necessary fat for harmless surgery when the resolution hits the floor but, beware, the house feminist will demand changing *man* to *humankind*. Also, enough layers of fat conceal the heart of the matter.)

And now the resolution is presented to the floor, along with thirty-seven others, by the chair of the resolutions committee, who begins the report by saying: "It is now five in the afternoon (actually, 5:10). I know you are all tired, and you will soon want to freshen up for the banquet. If I may have your indulgence, I will read the resolutions seriatim and expeditiously. I do hope you will give us your attention because my committee and I were up all night every night, and we think these resolutions deserve your careful consideration—for the next forty-five minutes." The chair then reads the first resolution and moves its adoption.

"Point of information, Mr. Chairman," barks a man at the middle microphone. "I'm Stanley Livstone, at mike number three, from Spokane, Washington. I have only one question: 'Is there a quorum present?'"

The chairperson, after hurried whispered consultations with everyone on the dais, explains that, according to the rules of the convention, a quorum consists of 50 percent of the people present, and "we will now proceed to vote on resolution number one." Mr. Livstone begins to appeal the chair's ruling, but his mike, which is controlled at the dais, goes unaccountably dead.

Mr. Livstone, after running madly from mike to mike looking for a live one, surrenders by the time the assembly gets up to resolution number ten (on anti-Semitic scrawling on subway ads). He gives up to go upstairs to freshen up. One by one, the other delegates shuffle out. The floor is emptying. As the exodus increases, the chair hits the panic button and reads faster, determined to hit the finish line before the stenotypist and parliamentarian go catatonic. As the buzz of the departing delegates rises, the chair tears through the resolutions in staccato barks like a tobacco auctioneer. Enough with the seriatim: "I have here a resolution on better service to chapters. Who's for it? Do I hear a second? Good. Do I hear any objection? It is so ordered. I have here a resolution on the perpetuation of the Jewish people. Who's for it? Second? Objection? So ordered. I have here a resolution on Communism. Who's against it . . . etc., etc.?"

And so the report of the resolutions committee is adopted, and the course of the organization is charted for the next year. Before pounding the gavel for adjournment, the chair turns to those associates at the front table (there are no more delegates in the hall) and proclaims: "I cannot refrain from expressing my deep gratitude to you and myself for demonstrating once again that we, the delegates, set policy in this organization in the best deliberative tradition of American democracy. We stand adjourned!"

Veterans of Jewish conventions, except for those who develop hernias from carrying the delegate's kit, have long since learned how to sleep with their eyes wide open, a look of eager earnestness fixed upon their faces. The pro rarely falls off his chair in the middle of a plenary session.

Appoint a Committee

This is the ultimate denouement, which justifies all that precedes. Jewish life without committees would be like lox without bagels or a men's club breakfast without a comedian.

If Moses had had a committee, the Ten Commandments would now be a draft document marked "Not for Publication," being "processed" by an editorial committee for "language" and subject to the veto of the separate boards of each tribe. The prophets could never have gotten their wild preachments through any committee. "Beat your swords into plowshares" would have come out of the wringer of the Prophetic Advisory Committee something like "wherever practicable, subject to national security and on an ad hoc basis only, earnest consideration should be given to the feasibility and desirability of converting swords, etc. . . . ."

Jews are unusually prone to committees. Nobody knows why. Perhaps for the same reason they are subject to ulcers. One of the most interesting types of committee is the *coordinating* committee, consisting of representatives from several organizations. Most representatives come to the meetings in order to check on the other organizations and to eat lunch.

Coordinators prepare agendas, call meetings, keep minutes, pass out sandwiches and seltzer, walk on eggs, play it by ear, get down to *tachlis* (the nitty-gritty), invest trivia with an aura of importance, circulate pink confidential memoranda in advance of the meeting (marked "Destroy before Reading"), and try to keep the members of the committee from breaking up on the shoals of "philosophic differences," which, freely translated, means "Who does he think he is?" Votes are rarely taken. Things are decided on "the sense of the meeting," which means the chairman does what he and the coordinator want. Coordinating committees are powerful brakes against irresponsible action. This is achieved by the simple device of discouraging any action whatsoever. In extreme circumstances, where action erupts in spite of this careful process, a coordinator is hired to coordinate the coordinators.

Megalomania is inherent in organizational work. An exaggerated sense of our own power disguises the reality that we all function on the periphery of the margin, mostly unknown to either media or government and frequently even to our own constituents. Thus, in 1991, one national Jewish organization with an unpronounceable name and a barely visible membership (sustained mostly by its travel program) adopted a resolution calling for an early end to the Gulf War. Two days later, the war ended. The president of the organization FAXed his Board of Directors a message of self-congratulation and issued a press release of hallelujah that sounded very much as though he, God, and Schwartzkopf had jointly decimated the forces of evil.

To get the most out of a Jewish meeting, whether large or small, it is imperative to understand the vocabulary. The next chapter covers a glossary of frequently used terms with their real meanings.

3

A Glossary for Jewish Meetings

Here is a sampling of terms and definitions, providing a basic key to the *real* meaning of what is said at Jewish meetings:

We object to the manner in which this motion has been rail-roaded through. Meaning: We had it arranged for my side to put in our motion first.

I am sure that Mr. Berg has excellent authority to back his conclusion. Meaning: He doesn't know what he's talking about.

I don't question the sincerity of Mr. Stein's statement. Meaning: I question the sincerity of Mr. Stein's statement.

Mr. Glasser is a most devoted and tireless member of our board. Meaning: Mr. Glasser is a *nudnik*.

I don't think we should waste time going over the minutes of our last meeting. Meaning: Miss Klotznick never typed them.

Would you restate the motion? Meaning: They're not going to put anything over on me.

I had some remarks prepared for me by the staff, but I feel so close to this group I would rather just speak from my heart. Meaning: I will now make the remarks prepared for me by the staff.

My worthy colleague. Meaning: My worst enemy should have such a colleague.

I don't think we can take responsibility for the behavior of every individual Jew. Meaning: A Jewish *gonif* is on the front pages.

I think the entire Jewish community can take pride in the achievements of this great American. Meaning: A Jew has just won the Pulitzer Prize.

I think we must bear in mind the public relations implications of such a move. Meaning: Non-Jews won't like it.

I'm just talking off the top of my head. Meaning: I don't know what I'm talking about.

I don't recall the earlier comment, but I do believe . . . Meaning: I just woke up.

Let's set up a pilot project. Meaning: Let's kill it for a year.

I missed part of the meeting, but what I heard was most stimulating. Meaning: After I made my own comment, I fell asleep.

Let's adopt the idea in principle and have the exact language worked out later. Meaning: Let's kill this crazy idea and go home already.

Let's get down to *tachlis.* Meaning: (1) Let's change the subject. (2) Let's avoid a decision at all costs.

Why don't we leave these details to be worked out by the staff? Meaning: It's not important anyway.

The statement is wonderfully strong, but I think the committee should go over it. Meaning: It's too strong.

Would the waiters please clear the hall! Meaning: Here comes the pitch.

The previous speaker has already said much of what I had in mind, but it bears repeating. Meaning: He stole the only idea I had.

I will confine myself to a few brief remarks. Meaning: We'll be lucky to get home for "The Late, Late Show."

Can we keep this off the record? Meaning: The reporter is here from the *National Jewish Post.*

Will you withhold your applause until I have introduced all the people on the dais? Meaning: Everybody's on the dais.

Point of order! Meaning: Let me talk!

I'm glad to see the young people here because they are the leaders of tomorrow. Meaning: Who let all those kids in?

A token of our appreciation for his many years of unstinting and dedicated devotion to civic and Jewish causes . . . Meaning: Another plaque.

Speaking for myself, I'm very glad you brought that question up. Meaning: I was afraid some joker would bring that up.

Everybody who knows me knows that I strongly believe Jews should stand up and be counted. Meaning: Sometimes we have to rise above principle.

We all admire Mr. Shane Fergasson as a uniquely distinguished Jewish communal and civic leader. Meaning: He's a big giver.

We thank Herb for his most detailed and thorough report. He has certainly given us food for thought. Meaning: Let's eat already.

Mind you, I have no objection to the principle of this project, but I simply think we should carefully examine all the implications of it. Meaning: I'm against it.

Our committee has proceeded slowly and cautiously. Meaning: We haven't had a meeting yet.

I wonder if we could return to this point a little later. Meaning: Let's bury it.

I must say you have asked a very searching and challenging question. Meaning: I wish I knew the answer.

Nobody feels more strongly than I that Jews must be in the forefront of social justice. Meaning: Let's stay out of it.

Our decision to pool our efforts with those of all the other synagogues in the community in developing a joint communitywide program reflects our deep commitment to *K'lal Yisrael,* to the peoplehood of Israel. Meaning: This way we can split the costs.

There seems to be a general consensus in principle, and it remains only to work out the details. Meaning: It's hopeless.

Look, before we go rushing into something, why don't we conduct a survey so we know where we stand. Meaning: Let's kill this *meshuggeneh* idea.

I don't mean to cut you off. Meaning: You've had it.

There has been an outpouring of protests across the country. Meaning: Two letters, one postcard.

Look, I can live with this. Meaning: I have a choice?

The staff can clear up the language. Meaning: So we can say it like we mean it, not like we said it.

I take your point. Meaning: I don't always agree with what I say.

Exactly what do we want to get out of this? Meaning: Me.

Max, our staff director, has been tireless and devoted, a giant in this field, and his contribution over the years has been beyond calculation. Meaning: Our Max is a goner.

JNF has appropriately honored our guest. Meaning: They cut down six hundred trees in his honor.

I think there's a light at the end of the tunnel. Meaning: Yeah, but it's probably an oncoming locomotive!

(The original version of this glossary was written jointly with Paul Kresh.)

4

The Pope Is Coming, the Pope Is Coming

The purpose of the meeting was simple: the Pope was planning a visit to the United States and graciously requested a meeting with representatives of the Jewish community at the very first stop on his itinerary. He would, of course, leave it to the Jewish leaders to determine the person to respond for the Jews.

Could anything be simpler? All that had to be done was to call a meeting of representative Jewish leaders to work it out well in advance.

Here are the minutes of that apocryphal (we should live so long) meeting:

Rabbi Cohen: "Okay, we all know why we are here. So I call the meeting to order."

Mr. Fram: "Who authorized you to preside? Why the Synagogue Assembly and not the Council of Lesser Organizations or another umbrella? No one organization has the right to convene us. This should be a nonauspices meeting."

"Okay, okay, it's nonauspices. I'll cancel the coffee my organization was going to serve. Let's deal with the substantive question. Who will speak for the Jews in the meeting with the Pope and what will he say?"

"You mean he or *she*," said Tillie, the house feminist.

"Never mind *she*," said Rabbi Levy. "Stop with the gender

mishegoss. The question is what we should say to the Pope on this historic occasion."

"Wrong question," shouted Rabbi Levy. "The question is *Why* should we meet with the Pope altogether? Because he wants a party? *Mazel tov!* My organization doesn't dance at every wedding. We find it demeaning to accept the Pope's fait accompli. Who is he to tell us where, when, how many minutes? Where is our dignity? Are we ecumaniacs? Were we consulted on the agenda?"

"Come off it, Hesh! Here's the Pope of Rome, visiting the United States. He has asked to meet with the Jewish community at his first stop. Considering our terrible history, isn't that progress? Is it impossible for you to take yes for an answer?"

"What progress?" demands Levy. "He met with Arafat; he refuses to recognize Israel. Now he gives us fifty minutes. Big deal! Hardly time to say—*gut yontiff,* Pontiff!"

"Wait, wait, wait," cried Tillie Ginsberg. "The question is not *should* we meet him. How can we *not* meet him? Are we a ghetto community? The question is *who* speaks? I suggest it should be a distinguished woman! That in itself will be a more eloquent statement than . . ."

"*Narrishkeit,* utter nonsense," exploded Berl Isaacson. "I have no doubt what distinguished woman Tillie has in mind. No, Tillie, it must be a rabbi—male, Orthodox, and with a yarmulke—to demonstrate we are a Torah community, proper peers to the Church and not mere secular Jews."

"Not so fast," exploded Davidoff, a prominent Reform lay leader. "We are not a singular community but a plural one— indeed a many-splendored people, including Reform, Conservative, Reconstructionist, and even secular. . . ."

"What *even?*" exclaimed Mike Fink, executive of a national Jewish defense agency. "We Jews are not only ecclesiastical, we are also civic and communal. The Jewish speaker could come from any of the streams and strands that make up the fabric of Jewish life. Why do we have all these umbrella organizations if not to help us out on a rainy day? We propose a lottery! Put all our presidents in a hat and draw!"

"A lottery!" hissed Fram. "Demeaning! A travesty! Is this Purim? Is this a game? Look, we'll tell the Pope and the world we cannot agree on a single spokesman and that's that!"

"Not *man! Spokesperson!*" shouted Tillie.

"So let's tell him," Rabbi Cohen said, "we couldn't agree on one person. So instead, when he finishes speaking, we'll treat him to the War of the Jews—twenty separate statements leaping from our various smoking mimeograph machines right into *The New York Times.* Let him read our response in the *Times.* Is *that* what we want?"

This gave everybody pause. How would it look? What kind of public relations? Is it good or bad for the Jews?

"Personally," said Isaacson, "my organization will not attend this meeting with the Pope under any circumstances."

"Mine either," chimed in Rabbi Levy. . . . "We wouldn't go. . . ."

"Well," said Davidoff, "mine will be there, no matter what, because we believe there has been more progress in the twenty-five years since *Nostra Aetate* than in all the centuries before, and we intend to celebrate that. . . ."

"What's a Nostertata?" whispered Fram.

"And don't celebrate," said Levy, ignoring Fram. "Acknowledge maybe, but don't celebrate."

"Anyway, we'll be there, that's for sure," Davidoff said, "even if we are the only Jewish group. In fact, *especially* if we are the only Jewish group. This will be a major media event, our dialogue with the Pope."

"Wait, if you Reformers are the only Jewish organization there, it would be a double disaster. Our people don't like the Pope, but they like you even less. So if you go, we'll go too, under protest, to checkmate you," said Cohen.

"If you, then we too, to keep an eye on you, the sister organization in our own movement," said Levy.

"Why sister? Could also be brother," murmured Tillie, spilling her tea in exasperation. "You people are anti-Christian and sexist, and you do not speak for the Jews. . . ."

"Time out from fighting," said Fram. "I have a Pope story. Seems President Bush had an audience with the Pope and, in casual conversation, asked the Pope how many people work in the Vatican. The Pontiff paused a moment and replied: 'About half, I think.' "

"About the same percentage in my organization," said Levy.

"Cut out the nonsense," said Isaacson. "We have to pick somebody. I say that person must come from one of our agencies that deals professionally with interfaith relations. This must not be amateur night. As it happens, my agency . . ."

"Baloney," interjected Levy. "Again with the turf. Forget the turf. Let's just pick the person most qualified, *ad personum,* regardless of agency. Merit, merit should be the only criterion. And, therefore, I propose . . ."

"I propose," cut in Isaacson, "that you get real. Are you kidding? What planet do you inhabit? In the real world, turf and credit are the names of the game, so please do not hock us about merit, whatever that means."

"But who should be the Jewish speaker, already?" Fink demanded.

"Look, Fram," mused Levy. "*Nostra Aetate* in Hebrew means if you don't know where you are going, any route will take you there."

The upshot was, as always, the appointment of a subcommittee. On the appointment of a subcommittee that, if it meets at all, will figure out how to lose the problem one way or another, the Jewish leadership maintains a virtual unanimity.

5

How to Escape Jewish Fund-Raising (You Should Live So Long!)

News Item: More than six hundred Jewish leaders attended a black-tie dinner last night at the Waldorf-Astoria in New York, launching the United Jewish Appeal campaign. The minimum contribution for the event was $10,000. So many persons demanded to attend that the UJA had to move the dinner from a small ballroom at the Hilton to the Grand Ballroom at the Waldorf. . . .

This actual event, by no means extraordinary in fund-raising, confirms what all Jews—and many non-Jews—already know: American Jewry has turned fund-raising into an art. In 1967, in a matter of weeks after Israel's Six Day War, American Jews raised a half-billion dollars. Jews give some $625 million to Jewish causes every year. In the 1990s Jewish fund-raising for the historic Soviet resettlement will produce billions of dollars. It seems that Jews regard giving to charity as not merely philanthropic and Pavlovian but as a biblical injunction. Add this age-old commandment to the never-ending story of Jewish heartbreak and you can understand why Jews are such easy marks.

Jews are masters at the fund-raising game. Capturing the big givers is like a bullfight. Everybody knows that in the end the bull will bleed. But the excitement lies in the pageantry and in the skill of the match: the veronica passes, the feints, the flourishes, the footwork, the timing. The two or three great matadors of Jewish fund-raising inspire awe; they are living legends. How do you recognize one? If he phones you on your unlisted number to wish you a happy birthday, you might as well take out your checkbook on the spot. The game's over.

In Jewish fund-raising, the kill usually takes place at grand hotels, but the groundwork was laid much earlier in hundreds of encounters in country clubs and on golf courses, in offices and in elevators, on airplanes and in synagogues.

Here's the pitch: "Max, this is Hank. As I don't have to tell you, Israel is in trouble. Yes, again. I myself am doubling my pledge to the UJA. I'm counting on you to do it, too." Or "Bernie, this is Sid. Al Golden is one of your closest friends, isn't he? I thought so. We're having a dinner for him, and we are counting on you to increase your pledge in his honor. I'm sure you'll want to give at least as much as Max, who hates Al's guts. It's the least we can do for Al, right?"

Here's another: "Listen, Jack, Senator Whatshisname will speak at the dinner—he's the fan dancer—but what really counts are the pledges of the big givers to get the ball rolling. We're putting you down for $10,000. I know that's twice what you gave last year, but I bought $100,000-worth of goods from you, remember? We'll call on you first to get us off to a fast start. Thanks, pal."

Every spontaneous announcement at the Waldorf has been prepared with the meticulous care of an Apollo space launch. Sometimes there's a glitch, like the time Moish Hernberg pledged $5,000 in memory of the $25,000 he had contributed the year before.

Here are some ways (99 percent unsuccessful) to duck Jewish fund-raising:

Dissociate Yourself. This requires a blank look and a heart of wood. Don't let yourself be swept by Jewish emotion. But don't underestimate the downside of dissociation. Announcing that you are not interested, belong to no Jewish groups, or have absolutely no desire to contribute—these are all a waste of breath. To dissociate effectively you have to enter an FBI witness relocation program and adopt a new identity. Hiding anywhere in America is futile. A Jewish geography buff will sniff you out before you deplane. Try going abroad, but bear in mind that you can be extradited. The sun never sets on the UJA.

Say You Gave at the Office. This is a very common dodge, but it rarely works. The caller will already know how much you gave at the office, how much pain was applied, the effect upon your basal metabolism, how much you told your partner you gave, how much your partner told you he gave, how much you deducted from your income tax, and how long you take for lunch. Once an IRS agent in the Fraud Division called a rabbi and asked if he had an Arnold Schmuckler in his congregation. "Yes," said the rabbi. "And did this Arnold Schmuckler give $200,000 for the building fund of your synagogue?" Pause. "He will," promised the rabbi, "he will."

Stand on Principle. Denounce the entire campaign as contrary to the principles of equal justice. If your organization ran a deficit last year (and it did), say: "If God wanted us to live on a deficit budget, he would have made ink red instead of black. After all, why should a few of us (be sure to say *us,* not *you*) have to carry the heaviest burden of the campaign year after year, while several of the members who can afford to give much more than we can give peanuts?" The only way to remedy this injustice is to put the facts on the line! *"I'm* not embarrassed to publish my gift, and I would certainly like to know why anybody else should be embarrassed!" Wind up with a peroration: "Ladies and gentlemen, what are we trying to do here—give to save Jews or protect some fat cats among us from giving what they *should?"*

Then storm out of the room, saying: "I've had it up the gazoo! Count me out!" (This performance may win you an

Oscar, maybe even a reprieve of a few weeks. And you may pick up an extra plaque to sweeten your ultimate surrender. **Tip:** Before rushing out, make sure they didn't tie your shoelaces together and bolt the door.)

Wax Philosophical. This is a sophisticated gambit. Speak in a wise, weary voice, something like this: "Ladies and gentlemen, I'm as good a Jew as any of you, I think you'll have to admit. As you all know, I give $10,000 dollars anonymously every year. But times have changed. The day of sectarian giving is over. We live in an ecumenical, transdenominational era. Take Brandeis University. What's Jewish about it? The student body is nonsectarian, as it should be. So what's Jewish? The money? Why? Or take the Jewish Hospital. What's Jewish about it? It's open to everyone, regardless of race and religion. So what if it has a kosher kitchen? So does St. Joseph's Catholic Hospital. We've got to get rid of this sectarian system, starting with fund-raising. Why must I give as a Jew? Why not as a human being, an American, a compassionate person of the world? You see, ladies and gentlemen, I admire what you have done for so many years. But let's face it, in a modern welfare state, particularist giving is as anachronistic as animal sacrifices in the Temple."

A potent and intriguing argument will prevail until Esther, the chairwoman, fixes her gaze on you and says: "Okay, okay, Sam, very pretty, but it's a crock! You're as full of it as a Thanksgiving goose. So I'm putting you down for the same as last year." Your goose is cooked.

Become the Chair. As chair, you can try this ingenious escape route: "Being a chair of this campaign takes a tremendous number of hours. Figure out what my time is worth. That's my contribution—it's worth a fortune." It is a noble delusion. By the time the journal is in preparation, the pledges are being readied, and the screws are applied, you will not only give your time, but you will find yourself decked out in a shiny tuxedo at the big dinner, standing at the microphone in front of a four-tier dais, and announcing to an admiring throng: "As chair, and in tribute to the wonderful support you have all given me this year, I am proud to announce that I am doubling my pledge." Pandemonium. Applause. The old bar mitzvah glow all over again. And another ruse bites the dust.

Biblical Text. There is one other way—not to escape Jewish fund-raising exactly but at least to get your money's worth. The story is told of Mr. and Mrs. Jake Finegelt who, enjoying their summer vacation, visited the nearby temple. A fund-raising meeting was going on to secure funds for a new building. Each person filled out a pledge card and passed it up to the chair, who then announced it. A deeply loyal Jew, Finegelt decided to add his contribution. He made the pledge card out for $100 and passed it forward. "Isn't this nice," announced the chair, beaming. "Here's a wonderful couple, not even members, who are contributing to our building fund. **Mr. and Mrs. Finegelt pledge $500!"**

The Finegelts were upset, but they were too embarrassed to say anything after the congregation burst into applause. Finegelt rushed up later to protest. The chair apologized for the error, but he said Finegelt should have corrected him earlier. How would it look to announce the change now? Mr. Finegelt was not assuaged.

"Tell you what," said the chair. "Let's keep it at $500, and, to make it up to you, we'll put your favorite passage from the Bible over the entrance to the new building. Wouldn't that be an honor? That way, your gift will live forever. Just let me know which passage you desire."

Finegelt reluctantly agreed. He and his wife went back to their hotel and thumbed through the Bible. The next day they returned and supplied the text (now handsomely inscribed over the portal of a New England *shul*): "I came to you a stranger, and you took me in."

6

The Jewish Rubber Chicken Circuit

The Jewish lecture circuit is like every other lecture circuit—only more so. It has some uniquely Jewish components:

1. The superstars of the Jewish lecture circuit are, of course, non-Jews. The big fees do not go to Jewish lecturers. They go to non-Jewish political and media personalities, who become the centerpieces on the Jewish fund-raising circuit. Senators are big tickets, especially those who recite the most grandiose slogans about Israel ("that feisty bastion of democracy" . . . "our only real friend in the Middle East" . . . "a light unto the nations"). They do even better when they link these clichés with some tough talk about the dangers of the current administration policies toward Israel ("we must not substitute our judgment for Israel's—*they* know their security needs best").

If the senator comes from the same political party as the administration, his fee is worth an additional $2,000, especially if the event is a UJA or Federation gala fund-raising banquet. Such media stars as Bill Moyers, Dan Rather, Ted Koppel, Walter Cronkite, or Sam Donaldson are premium tickets, unless—like John Chancellor or Peter Jennings—they have said someting critical about Israel in recent years.

As for Jewish speakers, the sexy lecture tickets include people like Henry Kissinger, who are not too Jewish. The key to the speaker is the magnetic draw of his fame, not the speech (which will usually be a bland piece of boilerplate). If a nonfamous speaker spoke with the same monotone, he would be flushed down the toilet after his first outing. Kissinger, on the other hand, is good for a cool $20,000 a turkey on the chicken circuit.

There is only one way to beat the fee. Honor the speaker with your highest annual award, even if you invented it only this year. Who can refuse to come and accept your organization's magnificent *Ner Tamid* ("Eternal Light") Award, or the Medallion of the Golden Calf, or the *Kine Ahora* Prize for keeping away the evil eye? It is true that the speaker received a similar plaque from a church body, Our Lady of the Blessed Simchah, but what's wrong with a plaque on both your houses?

2. While the non-Jewish luminaries described in the first component listed above are always picked up in a chauffeured limousine by a welcoming committee of sycophants, the Jewish speaker at an out-of-town event is usually picked up by a luckless fellow who owes the rabbi a favor and who invariably forgets on which level he parked his car at the airport.

For all speakers, the actual lecture is the easiest aspect of the assignment. The most challenging is the socializing. Since he is being paid a fee, he is regarded as the choice property of the local committee from his moment of arrival until his departure. That means cocktails with the host committee; dinner with the officers; a private meeting with the big givers; a recorded interview on a radio program (which is heard at 6:30 A.M. on Sunday); a 7:15 A.M. breakfast meeting with the committee on long-range planning; and a whirlwind visit to the town's Jewish attractions: the country club, the olympic swimming pool at the Jewish Community Center, and the new temple and *mikveh* located twenty-seven miles out of town in the path of future Jewish migration. It is generally regarded as déclassé to inform the speaker in advance of these social events. The thought is that it is inhospitable and gauche to let him catch his breath in his hotel room (a Holiday Inn, of course). His lecture fee seems much too high if measured against an hour's lecture. Prorated over twenty-four hours of use, however, he is cheap at half the price.

3. When the speaker is traveling by car to a nearby speaking engagement, he is dependent on the host group's travel directions, which are, without exception, tests of intelligence and fortitude. These instructions always open with the words "You can't get lost; it's simple" and then proceed as follows:

"Get onto the Long Island Expressway (you will know it because it will be gridlocked at the hour you hit it; you should have arranged to beat the rush hour, which ends at 3:00 A.M.). Get off the LIE and proceed to the Cross Island Parkway (it may be called the Belt). I think it goes north and south. If so, you travel south; otherwise go west. Go over the Bronx-Whitestone Bridge (pay toll); exact change lane is faster. Get on the Hutch (watch out for speedtraps); exit at Mamaroneck . . . I'm not sure if it's Road or Avenue; there's both, but you will know it because there's a gray building on the right (if it's not too dark to see it). If you get to Connecticut, you've gone too far. Turn right and stay on Mamaroneck (Road or Avenue), whatever, until Ridgeway, which is three blocks before the light that appears suddenly after the third pothole and a large oak tree on the left. Bear left, but don't turn right; go up the hill. You'll see a K Mart, forget it, and on the right you'll see a building that looks like a Baha'i temple. It is. We are the building with the Greek columns just behind it and the Chinese restaurants on all sides."

These instructions never include the telephone number of the temple, so the speaker has to do original research when he realizes he is near the Meadowlands in New Jersey.

4. If the lecturer is Jewish, he will be least desirable and popular if he is a scholar. What a lecturer must bring is

humor, kitsch, and an instinct for the Jewish jugular—which is guilt. The lecturer who savages the listeners with a provocative and iconoclastic critique is a sure winner: "You are Jewish illiterates; you do not do enough for Israel; you have abandoned the blacks and the needy; you have failed Jewish education, Soviet Jewry, the Lubavitchers, the Jewish Federation, your dead ancestors, your cult-intoxicated children, your intermarried children, your elderly parents, your God, your synagogue, your Jewish patrimony." This attack on the Jewish *kishkes* is great therapy and high Jewish entertainment. The speaker who is guilt-edged and critical will certainly be asked back. **Warning:** If he is, perchance, a non-Jew and says the same things, he will, of course, be labeled an anti-Semite.

5. The latest cachet in Jewish lecturing is the scholar-in-residence, who is rented like a Hertz car with unlimited mileage for an entire weekend, beginning with a Friday evening Sabbath sermon and ending with a Sunday morning lecture, interspersed with thirteen occasions of local hospitality, ranging from tea to a live Saturday afternoon football game in the freezing rain.

The name is a misnomer. Scholars are poison. The pop lecturer is anointed as scholar because he has three speeches instead of one arrow in his quiver. He should be called *fresser*-in-residence. If he is not a big man (or woman) when he arrives, he will be by Sunday afternoon. He will have been fed (stuffed is more like it) a Shabbat dinner, cake at an *Oneg,* breakfast at "the Club," brunch at the temple, sandwiches at the sisterhood, lox and bagels at the men's club, deli with the youth group, (catered by the best kosher caterer [black] in town), watercress sandwiches and soggy tuna at the nearby church interfaith, not to mention baskets of wine, cheese, and fruit in his hotel room. If he doesn't consume these goodies voluntarily, they are applied intravenously by the hospitality committee.

The total value of the quality food (Jews eat simple but lavish) usually exceeds the value of the honorarium (which is a euphemism for a small fee).

6. The introduction—the speaker invariably receives a florid and excessive introduction, making him sound like a combination ancient Hebrew prophet and born-again Winston Churchill. How the speaker responds is the tip-off to his personality. He should be humorous at his own expense, gently self-deprecating. Some examples:

"Thank you. Your introduction sounds a bit more like an epitaph than a benediction."

"An introduction is like perfume: okay to sniff, but one shouldn't swallow it."

"As the introducer said, I need no introduction. What I need is a conclusion."

"After a lovely introduction like that, I can't wait to hear what I'm going to say."

"I feel like Adlai Stevenson, who was once told that his speech was so good, he should publish it posthumously, the sooner the better."

The Speech Itself

As one who has inflicted over six thousand speeches on masochistic audiences over the past forty years, I offer the following tips to anyone reckless enough to follow in my footsteps:

1. Beware of the question-and-answer period after your speech. That is the moment of ultimate vulnerability, when your victims get their best shot at your jugular. Make sure the chair permits only questions, no speeches. But what's to prevent your favorite hatchet man from perforating you like acupuncture in a long and personal tirade to which he adds: Is this not true?

One antidote is to accept the questions in bunches of three or four rather than *ad seriatim*. This way you can duck, finesse, finagle, shuffle, and pirouette in your response until the chair breaks in and announces that the *nosh* is getting cold and pushes you safely out the kitchen door to the outside exit.

2. Be prepared. Don't wing it. Write out your speech and write it yourself—don't monkey with ghosts. Remember the fate of the famous senator, widely admired for his masterful speeches, who became dependent on the young assistant who ghosted his speeches. Once, after the senator and his aide had a falling out, the senator arrived at the National Convention of Police Chiefs to deliver his keynote address on "Attacking Urban Crime."

So confident was he in his aide who had drafted the speech that the senator never bothered to read the text in advance. Soaring through his barn-burner on wings of rhetoric, the senator orated: "And now I will elucidate my ten-point plan for the eradication of crime." Oh, oh! The senator looked as if he were suffering meltdown, as he silently and incredulously read the next words of his text: *Okay, you pompous son of a bitch—you're on your own!*

3. Start with a nice, soft joke preferably at your own expense or, if not, one that mildly needles both the rabbi and the president of the congregation. For example: A Jewish man, a stranger to the congregation, appears in the receiving line of a large congregation with a famous rabbi. The stranger is accompanied by his ten-year-old son. "Rabbi, my young son here is thinking of becoming a rabbi. Naturally, since you are our role model, we drove a hundred miles today for him to meet you." The rabbi glows, puts his hand on the boy's head, and warmly says: "Son, I'm delighted you are considering the rabbinate. A sacred calling. Now that you are here, coming such a great distance to meet me, is there a question you would like to put to me?"

"Yes," the kid says. "When you are not up there making your speech, what else do you do?"

The rabbi removes his hand, grimaces ever so slightly, and says: "Look, kid, you don't want to be a rabbi. You want to be a temple *president!*"

4. When you ask the rabbi what you should speak about, he says about twenty minutes. If you do not strike oil in the first twenty minutes, stop boring. To keep track of time, put your gold watch ostentatiously on the top of the podium. There is a story of a non-Jew who was brought to the temple for the first time by a Jewish friend. "What does that mean?" the interested non-Jewish observer asked his friend. "Oh, that's the *Ner Tamid,* the 'Eternal Light,' which means the eternity of Jewish life. The scroll? What does that mean? That's the Torah, it means the Jewish law, the Five Books of Moses, respect for law. The wine cup? That's for *Kiddush,* the sanctification of the wine, to mark the Sabbath as a special day. And the watch the rabbi has just placed on the podium? Nothing, my friend, it means absolutely nothing."

5. What to do when the natives get hostile. One way is to cut your prepared speech to the bone, saying, "My address is 219 East 69th Street, New York City," and sit down. Or compensate for weak arguments with loud *shry*ing; or disarm the hecklers by inviting one to the microphone to state his objection; or tell them your "crazy kid" story, which goes like this and usually gets a hostile audience off the scent:

After the Shabbat service, the rabbi and the guest preacher stand at the receiving line to receive the *"gut Shabbes"* and "wonderful sermon" comments of congregants. But one young boy spurns the speaker's hand and says: "Lousy sermon. Worst I ever heard!" The rabbi almost *plotz*es with embarrassment, puts his arm around the speaker, and says:

"Don't get upset. This kid is off the wall! And, besides, *he only repeats what he hears everybody else say!*"

6. While it is true that the key to getting a good speaker is a fat fee, there are three other considerations that can overpower the fee question. Location, location, location. Knowledgeable speakers shrink from any engagement that requires changing planes, using the LIRR, flying in a tiny commuter plane, or taking the red-eye. They abhor facing the hassle of automobile traffic on Long Island, in New Jersey, Los Angeles, Miami, Houston, and many other metropolitan areas whose expressways grind to a roaring halt by 3:00 P.M. An invitation to join the rabbi for Shabbat dinner in any of these areas is greeted by the experienced speaker with all the anticipation of a request for a frontal lobotomy. Some very secularist Jewish speakers have become neo-*frumm*ies (zealous Orthodox) because it gets them out of a car and out of gridlock for twenty-four hours, thank God.

In recent years, conferences and conventions have been moved for convenience to airport hotels so people can zip in and out without disappearing into local traffic. This is much easier on all concerned, including the delegates, because the speakers are usually drowned out by jet noise.

EAT, EAT: Noshing Is Sacred

What unites the 57 varieties of Jewish functions where you may wind up speaking—brotherhood breakfasts, sisterhood collations, fund-raisers, and receptions—is one ingredient: food!

Jewish food always anchored the Jewish home. Why else do Chinese restaurants locate in Jewish neighborhoods? A scholar recently discovered that recorded Jewish history goes back four thousand years and Chinese history only three thousand. What is the significance of that discrepancy? It means that Jews survived for a thousand years without Chinese food. But food—Chinese, lox and bagels, *kreplach, tsimmis,* and the rest—puts zest into the Jewish home.

Now food is becoming the new rite of passage in Jewish institutions as well, particularly since the cost of eating in restaurants has gone off the scope. You want people to attend Shabbat services? Organize an *Oneg Shabbat* (a social hour after services) with shnecken, coffee, and tea. But beware of the new breed of Jewish bag ladies who appear like ectoplasm and deposit most of these goodies into their brown bags before you can say the *Motzi.* The *Oneg Shabbat* has become a major issue in the sunbelt (especially Florida) where hundreds of snowbirds, their faces tanned and their appetites honed, descend upon the *Oneg Shabbat* like barbarian hordes. Since the snowbirds pay dues to their congregations up north and not to the sunbelt congregation, where they winter, the costs for the sunbelt congregation tend to zoom. What to do? Some congregations now forgo the *Oneg Shabbat* spread, which often means that both the snowbirds and the natives forgo the religious service as well. Other congregations now station undercover guards, wearing black robes, disguised as assistant rabbis.

No self-respecting men's club can have a Sunday morning meeting without bagels and lox and eggs. No upwardly-mobile sisterhood can function without a donor luncheon of overboiled chicken. No interfaith dinner is worth its salt without soggy tuna and watercress sandwiches. No UJA event will fly without roast beef and pink sherbet in the ballroom of the best hotel in town. And no working meeting of a Jewish committee can make it without mountains of good Jewish deli. If a temple organizes an ambitious scholar-in-residence weekend, it takes a committee of fifty volunteers: one to call up the speaker and arrange the topics and forty-nine to plan, coordinate, arrange the centerpieces (and raffling them off afterward), and serve the seven meals around which the weekend is framed!

True, Jews tend to overeat, but they also follow every known diet fad, exercise manual, and Weight Watchers formula known to ballooning men and women. We spend half our lives overeating and half our lives dieting. That, one can say, reflects a realistic balance. Sitting down together to break bread is a Jewish delight. It reflects the wondrous sense of Jewish community. Getting up is something else again, but who ever said that being a Jew is supposed to be easy?

Your assigned topic and menu will also depend upon the ideology of the sponsoring group. National Jewish agencies were once fiercely different on ideological grounds. The American Jewish Committee was German Jewish, somewhat elitist and aristocratic, cool on Zionism, and it liked to work with "influentials" behind the scenes. The American Jewish Congress was hot on Zionism, mass-oriented, of Eastern European background, and given to strong public rallies and social action by the masses, and it wouldn't know an "influential" if it fell on one. The Jewish Labor Committee was Yiddish-speaking, Socialist, made up mostly of Eastern European immigrants, and hated influentials, especially if they were German Jewish capitalists. Etc.! Etc.!

Alas, time has washed away all these ethnic and ideological differences. Now they're all clones; membership is interchangeable. All are passionately pro-Zionist; the membership is American-born, regardless of ancient origins, and virtually nobody speaks either Hebrew or Yiddish.

Now they differ only in cultural nuance, and that means, primarily, food. Until the recession, the AJ Committee served an elegant dinner, with a free bar, good wine, hot hors d'oeuvres, and uniformed waiters. The AJ Congress served corned beef sandwiches on paper plates, with seltzer and cream soda. The Jewish Labor Committee served soggy salmon on onion bagels.

Now, since the recession, austerity has come to all Jewish agencies. Some Jewish organizations serve nothing but coffee.

The Synagogue Council of America provides hot water and tea bags. The NJCRAC (go explain—this is a small book) provides do-it-yourself menus for take-out.

Most invite you to brown bag it. Some offer limp egg salad, next to a box marked $10 for the lunch. The precipitous decline in the quality of food at Jewish meetings has also caused a steep decline in body count (attendance).

For what most Jews want to get out of a meeting is simply—themselves. It recalls the story of the Soviet apparatchik who ran into a colleague on the streets of Moscow: "Comrade, we missed you at the last meeting of the Politbureau." "Aha," said the apparatchik, "if I had known it was the *last,* I would have been glad to attend."

7

The Care and Feeding of the Rabbi

The unquestioned leaders of the Jewish community are the rabbis. They are preachers and pastoral counselors, ambassadors to the Gentiles, teachers and fund-raisers, ecumenicists and executives of the establishment. In congregations with building drives, they are architects, artists, and contractors as well. The rabbi is the *kolbonik,* the master of all trades for all seasons. Subjected to impossible and conflicting congregational pressures, they render a remarkable service to the Jewish and general community. Their prestige is high (although few of their people actually follow their lead). And, although they know in their hearts that congregants have given them their proxy insofar as prayer and Jewish learning are concerned, they persist in trying to lift the level of Jewish commitment and belief.

Rabbis come in four varieties: Reform, Conservative, Orthodox, Reconstructionist. The Conservative congregation is usually called a center; the Reform synagogue is usually called a temple. Thus it is that Conservative rabbis get bald at the center, and Reform rabbis get gray in the temple. But all rabbis have one hair-raising experience in common: the pulpit committee.

Charged with selecting a new rabbi, the pulpit committee combines the best traits of the Amazon headhunt, the Spanish Inquisition, and the American political convention. Its vagaries are both subtle and severe, as can be seen from the following purely fictional chronicle of one of the favorite indoor games of American Jews:

Temple Ohev Tsores, the largest congregation in Yeckville, has just lost its rabbi, who, unknown to the congregation, had his name placed on a "panel" of the Rabbinical Placement Committee. After rejections by thirteen other congregations, he has made a happy marriage with Temple Shir Chadash (which is Hebrew for "New Song" and is the invariable name taken by a temple after deciding it wanted a guitar-playing cantor, who would add Simon and Garfunkle songs to the ᵘ᾽rgy).

This caused much wailing, weeping, and gnashing of teeth among the leadership of Temple Ohev Tsores. Rabbi Bodek's defection made them forget that for the past seven years they had devoted their best energies to getting rid of that "who does he think he is." Indeed, one of the officers, who had waged a nonstop guerrilla war against him on the grounds that he was too political ("What does gun control have to do with religion?"), now insisted that the rabbi had no right to leave and threatened to take the matter to the Rabbinic Conference Ethics Committee.

No matter; the die was cast. The loss of Rabbi Bodek inspired a wave of retrospective admiration. People spoke of his charisma, warmth, and spirituality. ("Let's face it, we'll never have another rabbi like Bodek.") But now the future had to be attended to. A pulpit committee was named, and the most intensive search outside of Scotland Yard was on.

What does a pulpit committee look for? The exact opposite of the last rabbi. If the outgoing rabbi was flamboyant, charismatic, and spoke in tongues, the new rabbi will be dull as dishwater—ideally suited for a congregation that wishes to see the bland lead the bland. If the outgoing was a great preacher, the incoming is sure to be pastoral. If the outgoing was successful with the youth group, this one will score with the yuppies and the guppies (geriatric-uppity). If the outgoing was big on social action, the new one will be housebroken, domesticated, preferring the "spiritual to the political," and will wear a knitted yarmulke.

(A rabbi in search of a pulpit should not apply to succeed a great rabbi. That successor is doomed to fail by invidious comparisons, even if Congregation Vasuch Vus didn't confer greatness upon their emeritus until the retirement banquet. Better to follow the rabbi *after* the rabbi who succeeded the great rabbi. Then—and only then—can you be secure enough to palm off a *nudnik* board member, who wants you to officiate at the intermarriage of his daughter six months hence, by telling him: "Oh, March 16 of next year? So sorry, I have a funeral that day.")

The committee at Ohev Tsores ponders: What kind of rabbi do we want? Young or old? Hot or cold on social action? Male or female? Attractive or not too good-looking? They agreed only that the rabbi should be married; neither too young nor too old (forty is too old); a good preacher, but for no more than twenty minutes; a good mixer; a regular fellow (should be able to listen to an off-color joke, but not tell one); a hard worker; an effective teacher (mostly for the kids); and a fine representative to the Christians.

Now come the candidates, one by one. Although they couldn't be more diverse physically, they sound remarkably alike: "I will insist on raising the standards of the religious school . . . Adults must learn . . . Judaism is not a juvenile religion, you know . . . I can't visit you unless I know you're sick . . . My pulpit will be a free pulpit . . . I can't do it alone . . . Judaism has to be relevant to modern life; it's not a shrine for a dead past."

The questions start slowly but soon are pitched with vigor: 50 percent curves, 25 percent fast balls, 25 percent bean balls. The rabbi, depending on his individual skill and previous experience with the banalities of pulpit committees, either takes the pitch, bunts, knocks it out of the park, or goes down swinging.

"Rabbi, would you officiate at an interfaith wedding?" ("Absolutely no, but, on the other hand, circumstances . . .")

"How do you feel about rabbis of the gay persuasion?" ("I'm for equal rights, of course, but we must not neglect Jewish tradition.")

"Tell me, Rabbi, do you consider yourself a Zionist?" ("Yes, but what do you mean by Zionist? Now that there is a State of Israel, etc.")

"Do you think the rabbi or the board should lead?" ("It should be a partnership. . . .")

"Would you object to a temple bowling league?" ("As a person who enjoys sports, no, but I have doubts about the Jewish significance of bowling.")

"Do you go around changing God from His to Her?" ("I'm all for gender equality, but, on the other hand, . . .")

"Should Hebrew play an important role in the school?" ("I feel that Hebrew is important. On the other hand, here in the Diaspora . . .")

"Do you speak on political issues?" ("Well now, what do you mean by 'political'? You know sometimes we must rise above principle.")

"What would you do to stimulate attendance at services?" ("Encourage leaders like you to attend regularly.") Murmur of discontent.

"I hope this isn't indelicate, but what about your wife? Will she play an active role in the sisterhood, for example? And, by the way, do you happen to have a snapshot of your wife in your wallet?"

Finally, months later, the course is run. The rabbis most desired prove unavailable or no longer interested, and the choice comes down to Rabbi Parveh, who neither offended nor excited a single member of the pulpit committee. In presenting him to the congregation for the first time, the president says:

"And you can be assured we combed the country from East to West to find the best suited rabbi to fill this pulpit so capably held for seven years by our beloved Rabbi Bodek. The pulpit committee never doubted for a moment that Rabbi Parveh was just the spiritual leader for whom we were looking. He is our unanimous and enthusiastic selection, and we present him to you with our prayerful gratitude to the committee for a hard job brilliantly done."

Rabbi Parveh turned out to be a first-rate rabbi, despite his having to fend off occasional needling and sniping from a small group of malcontents—all of whom, of course, had been members of the pulpit committee.

Whack the Rabbi

Whack the Rabbi is the Jewish equivalent of shooting fish in a barrel. It is a game played in every synagogue of every branch of Judaism. Usually it is harmless; sometimes it is vicious. Its universal appeal remains a psychological mystery, but it may have something to do with the guilt feelings Jews harbor for making the rabbi their religious surrogate. Perhaps it's a latent anti-rabbinism with roots in earlier generations. Maybe it's sublimation—we can't hit our kids but, oh, the rabbi! Whatever it is, Jews seem to delight in the game of Whack the Rabbi.

Rules of the game:

Any number can play. Players are usually (but not always) members of the synagogue. It is not considered good form to Whack the Rabbi of another institution; that's poaching. It is regarded as bad sportsmanship to Whack the Rabbi during the first three months (the honeymoon) or the last three months of his or her tenure (lame duck). The rabbi is fair game at all other times.

Here are some examples of whacks:

The rabbi greets you warmly on the reception line after Sabbath services: *"Gut Shabbes,* nice to see you." You respond with an inside double whack: "Glad to see you, too, Rabbi, but where were you when I was home with a broken leg?" Or: "Wassamatter, Rabbi, you don't make house calls? I mean, after all, I *am* one of your rare admirers."

The rabbi makes a plea from the pulpit for more generous U.S. foreign aid. You greet the rabbi in the receiving line: "Rabbi, tell me, What is your experience in international economics and geopolitics?" And, before the rabbi can respond, you cross with a whack to the jaw: "And when are you going to stop preaching about social justice and start talking about Torah?"

The rabbi takes a strong public position against a pot bust at the local college. It is carried on page one of the local newspaper under the headline: "Rabbi Says Get Off the Pot!" This affords you a great opportunity to deliver a public whack, which, among those who play the game best, is regarded as twice as valuable as an inside whack. You write a letter to the newspaper: *"The Rabbi Does Not Speak for Me!"*

The temple board is locking horns in a controversy about the new building plan. The rabbi expresses his opinion. You can, if you are not alert, pass by the rabbi's comments. But, if you are quick, you can slip in an effective whack: "With all due deference, Rabbi, I think this is a business matter. . . ." Then the business *mavens* can proceed, without jurisdictional confusion, to bankrupt the temple.

The rabbi is confined to a hospital bed after an appendectomy, and the president of the congregation visits him and announces beamingly that he brings the best wishes of the Board of Trustees, as expressed in a resolution adopted just last night by a vote of seventeen to twelve.

"Rabbi," says the president of the youth group, "I loved being at camp this summer. Really turned me on! Those rabbis are real swingers, running around in their bermudas, strumming guitars, and singing songs into the middle of the night. [Pause] You've never been to camp, have you, Rabbi?" . . .

Crack the Whack

No rabbi worth his salt will take his whacks lying down. Veteran rabbis develop psychological armor of reinforced concrete. Coping with whacks and cracking them are challenges to a rabbi's self-respect and survival. While whacks are par for the rabbinic course, they can become too much to bear during the open season on rabbis (six months before contract renewal). If all else fails, however, the rabbi can issue a flaming statement on behalf of civil rights or against Christian silence, telling the press that the congregation cravenly attempted to muzzle the voice of prophetic Judaism, and leave town in a blaze of glory, a martyr to social justice, undeterred by a bunch of small-minded reactionaries. This is an ultimate crack the whack strategy, and it can hardly fail to win the attention of the pulpit committee of a larger congregation somewhere else. At the end of his itinerant career as a wandering Jew, the rabbi will be buried with this epitaph: *At last, a permanent position.*

Games Rabbis Play

Rabbis can fully relax only with other rabbis. Just as Jews generally are most comfortable with other Jews because only with them does one not have to feel like a Jew. (This works only in small groups; rabbinical conventions are another story.) Only with a colleague, over a social drink, a ripe joke, and juicy rumors of imminent pulpit changes, can a rabbi free himself or herself at least momentarily from the impossibly conflicting and exalted expectations of the laity. There are few lonelier persons than the rabbi in an isolated town, hundreds of miles from the nearest colleague. With whom can a rabbi talk? Lucky is the rabbi who can relax with a husband or wife, provided, of course, they are not sermon-judgers. No playwright likes to breakfast with a drama critic.

As the years since rabbinical seminary days stretch into the rabbinic menopause that refreshes, rabbis tend to wax increasingly nostalgic about the good ole student days. They become sentimental about colleagues in the class of '62, most of whom they couldn't abide as students. They become damp-eyed about the Hebrew Union College, where as students they organized sit-ins and revolts so militant as to make the Berkeley demonstrations seem as tame as a sisterhood fashion show.

After twenty-five years of service, rabbis receive an honorary doctorate from Hebrew Union College, leading one cynic to conclude: "When rabbis became doctors, that's when Judaism got sick!"

Rabbi Emeritus

The relationship between the new rabbi (he will be called *new* for at least twenty-five years) and the emeritus (the retired and/or burned-out rabbi) is a tangled and ambivalent web. Once in a while the relationship is good to the max. In one Canadian congregation, the emeritus boasted to a visitor that the relationship was perfect; indeed, he and his wife related to the "new rabbi" as to their own son. "Right," chimed in the wife of the emeritus, "we can't stand him."

Rabbinic Conference

There is no convention to equal a rabbinic conference. It may indeed be the most articulate assemblage in American life. To assuage the tender egos of those rabbis not invited to present papers, most rabbinic conferences have now added preconference and postconference sessions to allow a larger number of rabbis to inflict upon each other the pearls of their sermonic repertoire. (Of course, the title is changed from "For Such a Time As This" to "A Teleological Analysis of Buberian Mysticism in the Light of the Maimonidean Synthesis.")

Plenum competitiveness and hyperbolic escalation run rampant, but even more fierce are the card games upstairs and the evil tongue lashing in the corridors. Rabbi X says to Rabbi Y: "Say, Rabbi Z told me that he gets an average of five hundred people to services every Shabbat. Is that possible or is he exaggerating?"

Replies Rabbi Y: "Well, I've been to Rabbi Z's services several times. I would say he averages about three hundred people every Friday."

"Hmmm," says Rabbi X, "so he's not exaggerating."

The rabbi is the chief target and the main hope of American Jewish life. And largely responsible for his or her becoming one or the other are synagogue lay leaders, those usually devoted, sometimes sensitive, sometimes insufferable professional volunteers who themselves live in the fishbowl of Jewish community life. . . .

8

They Make You Gray at the Temple or Bald in the Center: The Cast of Characters

Label the Characters

MACHER (Top Gun)

KOCHLEFFEL (Gossip)

NUDNIK (Pest)

NEBBISH (Sweet Nothing)

SHLEMIEL (Fool)

YOUNG MARRIEDS

A.K. (ANCIENT KNIGHT)

POTENTIAL LEADER

LEADER (Macher)

Few Jews can be pigeonholed into one of the above categories, but every chapter, club, lodge, or temple has such a cast of characters. The relative distribution of this share determines the character of the institution.

MACHER is an important lay leader. She is a leader by virtue of her influence, dedication, and/or affluence. She is often the big giver to the building campaign and announces the same pledge publicly as often as possible. (Unlike K [see Kochleffel below], she even pays it.)

Despite her limited knowledge of Judaism, she is tenaciously loyal to the organization and works harder for the cause than for her own business. She loves Jewish life and is hurt and distressed that her college-age son dismisses Jewish life as "vulgar and bourgeois." When her son marries out of the faith, she is humiliated and blames her husband; when the daughter-in-law converts and becomes a leading light of the sisterhood, she *kvell*s (beams) and takes full credit. M has been to Israel ten times and has cried every time. She is a pillar of Jewish survival.

She regards the rabbi and the rabbi's family as the property of the temple. When the rabbi buys a new Lincoln, M says: "We don't need the rabbi to be too fancy!" You can always tell who the *macher* is because the rabbi always publicly praises her as indefatigable, dedicated, zealous, consecrated, and beloved. How the rabbi describes her privately can only be imagined.

KOCHLEFFEL is the man (or woman) who stirs things up by the use of gossip, exaggeration, rumor, and innuendo. By definition, a *kochleffel* is a threat to the establishment. Say that Congregation Judea has just retained a young, unmarried rabbi, Kochleffel will whisper to Mrs. Paramount News (the eyes and the ears of the temple): "A nice boy, but what kind of a Jewish boy is unmarried?" Mrs. Paramount News takes it from there.

No American is more vulnerable than an unmarried male rabbi in a congregation. He must run an obstacle course consisting of every unwed Jewish girl in town, everybody's niece, and every lonely Jewish widow within a radius of three hundred miles until, in exhausted self-defense, he yields and takes a wife. When it is rumored that the rabbi is engaged to be married, our Mr. K asks at a men's club lox-and-bagel breakfast: "Is it true that the rabbi is marrying an Indonesian?" The truth is, of course, that the fiancée, Miss Ruth Ann Goldman, recently took a trip to the Orient. "Is it true that she has seven children by a previous marriage?" This, too, is not true (she has seven brothers and sisters), but the telephones leap throughout the community for days.

The wedding finally takes place at the temple. It is a joyous event, and the congregation is ecstatic. Except for K: "To me she looks already pregnant." If K is powerful as well as mischievous, he will ultimately: (1) drive the rabbi out of the temple, (2) drive the president out of his skull, and (3) foment a split-off.

NUDNICK may or may not also be a *kochleffel,* but he or she is *always* a pest. N is always certain to correct the minutes; test the rabbi ("You remember me, Rabbi, what's my name?"); refuse to pay dues to the parent national body; bring Robert's Rules of Order to the annual meeting; refuse to make the election unanimous; hold up the Shabbat evening receiving line (by telling the rabbi: "There are several points in your sermon I would like to discuss with you"); write monthly letters to the temple bulletin editor ("Either the Christian choir goes or I go!"); and at every opportunity ask: "Who authorized that?" If in league with K and A.K. (see below), N is a menace. Otherwise, he or she is just a pest and a living witness to the group's toleration of dissent.

NEBBISH is a sweet nothing. He or she is certain to smile uncomplainingly no matter what the disaster on all sides; approve everything; serve as chairperson of the committee on time and place; raise his or her voluntary dues voluntarily on the strength of one telephone call; pick up all the stuff for the bazaar in a new car; drive the speaker to the hotel; read the temple bulletin from cover to cover twice; listen to everything K says but fail miserably to pass it on, thus breaking the chain of communication; second the motion; and belong to both temples when the split comes.

SHLEMIEL is a fool, not dangerous like K or pesty like N or passive like Neb but unwittingly and unfailingly gauche. He is certain to drop the prayer book in the middle of the rabbi's sermon; complain that he came to services, but it isn't his night to usher; table the motion when he meant only to get the subject on the table; lose the speaker only six blocks from the temple; drive the youth group to the ballgame and forget where he parked the car; schedule the bowling tournament on the afternoon of Yom Kippur; blow out all the lights in the temple when changing a fuse in the middle of the drama group's presentation of *Fiddler on the Roof;* and fall off the *sukah* (the booth for the festival of Sukot) and break his second leg (the first he broke at a rally for Soviet Jewry when he foolishly marched off by himself in the wrong direction and fell into an open manhole).

Shlemiel should not be confused with a *shlimazel.* When Shlemiel spills hot tea, the *shlimazel* is the one he spills it on. When the *shlimazel* buys a suit with two pairs of pants, he burns a cigarette hole in the jacket. The *schlimazel* is a nice person if only he can be kept in his place—which is home, locked in his bedroom.

YOUNG MARRIEDS are a special breed of temple members, too old (old is your age plus ten) for the youth group and too young to die. Their principal identification with the temple is that they work hard at being youthful and married. A certain exclusiveness marks this group. They do not like unmarried people around; it makes them nervous. They do not like old people around either, especially if they are younger than the YMs themselves. Dancing, singing, discussions, weight watching, dramas, and trips to Bermuda keep the YMs young and carefree. The YMs can absorb one K and one S, but more than that would set wives and husbands at one another's throats and disrupt the entire program.

A.K. (ANCIENT KNIGHT) is a person long since over the hill—but unwilling to surrender. A.K. may well have been an M for a long time—and may be one still—but he may also develop the attributes of a K and an N in his older years. A.K. may also be in the first stages of senility, forgetting that he is only the honorary president emeritus and not the regnant knight. Why is this knight different from all other knights? Chronological years have nothing to do with it. A.K. is often a forty-one-year-old ex-*shul* president. He has a tantrum any-time his name is not mentioned at an open meeting, threatening to cut the temple out of his will and boycott the temple cemetery.

POTENTIAL LEADER is a person, preferably a yuppie, who is dynamic, articulate, knowledgeable, intellectual, and well fixed. The only quality lacking in PL is some interest in our organization (a lost leader). Many organizations have tried leadership training, bringing PL to luncheon sessions where the techniques of group dynamics and motivation research are utilized in a dazzling succession of socio-dramas, sensitivity courses, open-ended discussions, free association, and institutional half-nelsons. All these modern techniques prove that the only way to make PL an M or an L (Leader) is through *koved* (which means, roughly, feeding her ego). *Koved* consists of: (1) naming something permanent (like the rabbi emeritus) after her; (2) making her Woman of the Year or, if necessary, of the century; (3) putting her picture in the newspaper; (4) mentioning her in every issue of the temple bulletin; and (5) putting her on the board of the parent organization. If you cannot make an L out of a PL, you may have a potential K or N on your hands until she is old enough to become a YM and/or an A.K. If you succeed in making a leader of her, make a Xerox of her before she is stolen by the local welfare fund and FAXed to the big givers.

The LEADER in Jewish life, whether a paid professional or a dedicated lay volunteer, has as his or her primary tasks the disbursement of *koved* (read patronage); the involvement of lay people (read manipulation); and the achievement of the true goals of the organization (read blood, sweat, and tears).

Typical Ls are in their mid-forties, married, with two and a half children, a Buick with a dented front fender, and a three-bedroom ranch house in the suburbs, near transportation. They have a flare for anonymity and do not mind (they hate it, really, but keep it to themselves) writing eloquent speeches and reports that are ultimately delivered by some prominent lay *macher* as his own. They attend five meetings a week, at three of which they eat corned beef on rye off a paper plate and drink Dr. Brown's celery tonic (recently replaced by diet colas) during ideological discussions (read: which organizations should get credit).

Typical Ls had, as children, seven or eight years of Jewish education, not quite enough to extinguish all spark of Jewish interest. They are and have always been idealists and have no head for business. One L took over his father's successful mortuary and worked it into the ground in six months. As a boy he dreamed of being a kibbutznik in Israel or the first Jewish president of the United States. As he got older, his aspirations rose.

How successful a Jewish organization or temple will be depends on how the pieces, described above, are deployed across the institutional chessboard. The A.K., who can move only one space at a time, should not be counted on for the attack. K moves laterally and backwards and should be surrendered early for an opposing piece. N, YM, and Neb are mere pawns. S can hurt you if you're not careful. M, who moves like a queen, in all directions, has the power to lead the attack. PL must be moved forward rapidly and crowned, if at all possible. L, who moves like a horse, two-steps one way and one the other, can be very helpful if he or she is not exposed too soon and conquered.

9

Jews and Politics: The First Jew in the White House

All this wistful talk of General Colin Powell as a possible vice-presidential or maybe even presidential candidate has got me thinking. Now that we've had a Roman Catholic president, a divorced president, a born-again Southern president, are we ready for a black? A woman? A Jew?

Last night I dreamt that a Jew became president of the United States. It all began at the political convention in 2004, in Candlestick Park, San Francisco. The front-runners had faded out, including Senator Al Gore who was rapidly becoming the Harold Stassen of the twenty-first century. Even the most obvious dark horses like Pete Williams of the Pentagon had fallen by the wayside in the marathon balloting, when the name of Jacob Meyer, the young (forty-two), popular mayor of Minneapolis, emerged out of nowhere. A Jew! Dare we nominate a Jew? Can a Jew be elected? The whispered questions swept through the tense assembly. The fortieth ballot began. Suddenly, Jacob Meyer received an urgent note asking for an immediate private meeting with the leaders of the American Jewish Human Relations Council.

Leaving his seat, Meyer met the Jewish group in a secluded room in the basement. (It turned out later that three other Jewish organizations were waiting in three separate rooms with three different views to express, but he didn't know it.)

The head of the organization, a distinguished banker from Memphis, placed his hand on Meyer's shoulder and said: "Jacob, we know how tempting it must be for you to go for this nomination. It is a great honor. But, Jacob, we urge you not to do it. You will open the floodgates of hatred. Remember what happened to Al Smith and John F. Kennedy? Well, what they would do to you would make those campaigns look like communion breakfasts. Heaven knows what they would do to you—and to us. The anti-Semites will creep out from under every rock. We fear pogroms. Please, Jake, think carefully before you do this thing." Mr. Meyer promised to think about it, and he really did—right up to the moment when Governor Arm of Pennsylvania swung his delegation to Jacob Meyer, thus assuring Meyer's nomination for the presidency of the United States.

The next morning Meyer received a telegram from that same Jewish organization, hailing his nomination as a "triumph of the American dream that neither religion nor race is a barrier to public office." The telegram also asked him to endorse the organization's statement that there is no such thing as a "Jewish vote" and that Americans vote solely as Americans. Summoning his assistant, Meyer said: "Brady, send them a telegram telling them I endorse their sentiments completely and that they are rendering a fine service to the American people. Then get Herb, Mossy, and Pat on the telephone and tell them to go to work on the Jewish voters in New York, California, Florida, and Illinois. I need 90 percent in those key states or I'm a dead *kotchke.*"

There was, as predicted, a good deal of nastiness in the campaign that brought Meyer to the presidency. One hundred leaders issued a manifesto, raising the "religious issue" in the election. Could he dine in the Kremlin or even the United Nations or would he have to bow out of important negotiations because they serve shrimp? Could he enforce the Humane Slaughter Act without discriminating in favor of cows and poultry and against pigs and lobsters? Would he be even-handed with Israel? (The Israelis were sure the answer would be no and started a campaign to draft Reagan again.)

Would he place a *mezuzah* on the doorpost of the White House? Would he light the Christmas tree in the White House? Would he work and travel on Shabbat?

Meyer took to television, saying: "My Jewish faith will have nothing, I repeat nothing, to do with my presidency. Any conflicts between my Jewishness and my Americanism, I assure you, would be resolved in favor of my oath and responsibility to all the people." This eliminated the religious issue except, of course, in one segment of the American public: the Jews. The English-Jewish press boiled over with agitated editorials on how Meyer "has leaned over so far backward he has fallen on his behind" and "Is Meyer a self-hater?" One excitable communal leader told a startled reporter that he regarded Meyer as an outstanding "anti-Semite." The reporter gulped momentarily and said: "But Meyer is Jewish!" "Aha," shot back the leader, "that's the worst kind."

So Jacob Meyer became the first Jewish president of the United States. Although Meyer ran a scrupulously ethical administration, it was not long before there was rumbling about the president's "kitchen cabinet." (One wag said a Jewish president should have two "kitchen cabinets," one for milk and one for meat.) As it happened, the one "kitchen cabinet" consisted of the president's cousin Charlie, who had never been able to hold down a job anywhere and now became the president's appointments secretary; and, of course, Bubbe Meyer, the president's extraordinary eighty-eight-year-old immigrant grandmother (quickly named "Bobby" by the Hearst press, which slyly suggested she had taken over the White House, portraying her as a cross between Rasputin and the Wicked Witch of the West); the president's bewildered wife, Sally (about whom the Yiddish press asked what kind of name that was for a Jewish girl); and his fifteen-year-old son, Hiram, and twenty-five-year-old daughter, Deborah, both of whom had to be lifted bodily from their beds every Saturday morning to be marched to the synagogue with the family for the waiting photographers. The synagogue-going didn't help much because, when the Lubavitchers found out it was a Reform temple, they recited *Kaddish* for his Jewish soul before the CNN camera.

President Meyer's administration served at a time of great tension. The cabinet frequently met around the clock. Being dedicated and patriotic Americans, they did not mind the heavy burden of their tasks. What wrecked them in the end was the incessant airlift of sandwiches flown in daily from the Stage Delicatessen in New York City. As Secretary of Agriculture Baldwin said in his letter of resignation: "I did not mind that our meetings always started an hour late or that we had to go along with Grandma Meyer's silly plan to have a poster in every house saying Eat, Eat. What I could not take was another hot pastrami sandwich. My mind and spirit are still with you, Mr. President, but my stomach is shot."

Prior to his jet propulsion into politics, Jacob Meyer had been a partner in a flourishing drug store in Minneapolis. His partners had been a Roman Catholic named Aloyosius Kelly and a Methodist named Frank Holman. When he became president, Meyer found that Catholic organizations, seeking to reach the White House on a host of public matters, invoked the name of Kelly; Protestant groups made a conduit of Holman. Only Jewish groups had no contacts; so they, of course, were reduced to giving awards to Kelly and Holman. There was, of course, only one Jew in the cabinet. As Meyer confided to a friend, "If you wanted more Jews, you should have picked another Roman Catholic president."

President Meyer introduced unprecedented reforms into the government. A new and revolutionary committee structure was set up with every American assigned to a subcommittee. The president pushed through a constitutional amendment creating a vice-president in charge of fund-raising. While it was somewhat strange at first, the people soon got used to card calling whenever the budget had to be balanced. Indeed, voluntary contributions soon displaced the income tax. Techniques that had proved themselves in the United Jewish Appeal and the Israel Bond Drive soon began to work for the United States—except that the American Medical Association refused to turn over its mailing list to the government, foolishly charging that Bobby Meyers wanted to find out which doctors refused to make house calls. No one batted an eye when the president of U.S. Steel called the president of General Motors and said: "Give or else." Every trade and profession was organized for "crisis" giving; one hundred bankers gave $200,000 each year on condition that they would not have to go to fund-raising dinners, banquets, or "big-gifts" luncheons; and every taxpayer received a heartrending pamphlet annually, with pictures of starving children, dramatizing what would happen to America if contributions slackened.

The wives of members of Congress were organized by Sally and Bubbe into a United States Congressional Sisterhood, and a nationwide bazaar brought in more money than all excise taxes combined. Washington had never been livelier. All Supreme Court sessions were followed by a collation and entertainment. An *afikoman* hunt was cofeatured with Easter eggrolling on the White House lawn, and the summer White House was installed at the Fontainebleau in Miami Beach (until a visiting foreign minister got lost in the new wing and was forced to attend a workshop on "Small Congregations and Large Deficits," causing an international scandal). Presiding at a White House reception, beaming at the hoary senators whirling through the hora, passing out cigars, checking the stakes of the pinochle game in the East Room, keeping his guests' glasses filled with seltzer, Jacob Meyer became a beloved president.

Education was the theme of Meyer's administration. Not only was a college education available to every youngster, but it was compulsory. Adult education swept the country like Desert Storm.

"Other presidents like to throw out the first ball at the baseball game," President Meyer told Peter Jennings. "I would rather throw out the first question in the classroom." (Murmured Bobby: "Better you should talk to Dan Rather. Jennings I don't trust.")

A government TV network brought learning to every housewife. Teachers proudly admitted their professions. A football stadium at one university was turned into an open-air library. Colleges began giving scholarships to skinny, brainy boys with glasses, whom the prettiest coeds now clearly preferred to dumb, muscle-bound jocks. It was a new America—exhausting but exhilarating.

But, inevitably, a crisis came to the Meyer administration. It did not arise, as one might expect, in the tense international situation; hot tea and sponge cake had done much to drown the arms race and regional conflicts. The crisis was domestic. Grandma Bobby threatened to leave the White House, sending tremors through the nation's press. Robert Novak, maliciously predicting things to come, headlined: Queen Bee of White House Threatens Break with President over Food Policy; Calls President Too Thin, "He'll Get Consumption."

The true story is: It was *erev* Purim, 7:00 P.M. The entire Meyer clan had gathered for *hamantashen* and Purim dinner. The president said the *Motzi* blessing, and everybody began eating—except Grandma, who sat stone-faced and silent, staring straight ahead. "What's the matter, Bubbe?" asked Sally. "What should be the matter?" replied Grandma. She didn't touch a morsel. The president, an expert in domestic politics, felt the same sinking sensation that he experienced when he was about to beard Jesse Helms on civil rights. A storm was brewing. Dinner over, the president signaled everybody else out of the room and settled down to find out what was down-loading Bubbe's brain.

"Okay, Bubbe, I know you," he began. "Something's eating you. Now what is it?"

"What should be eating me?" she asked. "There's nothing eating me." Pause. "I'm leaving."

"Leaving the White House? Why, for heaven's sake? You're not happy here?"

She frowned darkly. "Okay, if you must know, I'm not happy."

The president, in spite of himself, found himself thinking in political terms. "Look, Bubbe, you can't leave. You're a key personality in my government. You get more mail than I do. The old people love you. You have a daily column in the Yiddish press. You've become a new-type Eleanor Roosevelt. If you leave me, the press will kill me with their wild speculations. Please!" He stared at her, seeing the familiar stubborn set of the chin. "Why? So tell me why?"

"In the first place," she said in the singsong fashion that suggested a long and telling list was coming, "I don't like the house. What do you need such a big house? It's a *shande* a man with such a small family should live like an Arab king! If the prophet Elijah tried to come to us for Pesach, he could not get through the cockamamy security system! You ask me, we should move into a nice, little ranch house with a picture window. And not in the middle of the city. In the suburbs, across the river in Virginia maybe. Barbara Walters wants to do me on Channel 7, but I'm ashamed she should come here. What Jewish family lives in the city?"

"Bubbe!" he cried out. "I'm the president. This is the White House. I've got to stay here!"

"What got to? Reagan lived in Santa Barbara and Carter at Camp David when he wasn't peanut farming in Georgia. And Bush in *yennavelt* in Maine. Why can't you live in a nice Jewish neighborhood in Arlington and play gin and send back the servants—who needs them? Sally can clean the house; she's not Queen Elizabeth or Imelda Marcos; and I could watch the soaps without the press and their daily pogroms!"

"That's ridiculous, Bubbe! You're a smart woman, why don't you . . ."

"And you, Jake, you should pardon me, you are a *shlemiel,* a twenty-five-karat *shlemiel.* All day and all night you work your fingers to the bone. Did you get a single raise? And the drugstore. So who is minding the drugstore; they're probably running it into the ground!"

"Bubbe, you're talking crazy."

"I'm crazy, eh? And you? Smart, smart, smart. And did you marry off your Debbie, already twenty-five years old? You should be ashamed—she's an old maid. You have a million people working for you, but one nice Jewish boy—he wouldn't have to be a doctor, his father could own a nice business—you couldn't find?"

"Please, please," said Jake, trying to dam up the flood. "You must realize . . ."

"And I'll tell you also, I don't like the people you have visiting here."

"People? Now what are you saying?"

"That Arab, whatshisname, with the *shmatte* on his head, you said I should be nice to him. A cossack, he should be boiled in oil. And the Polisher with the dirty beard, I thought he was a Lubavitcher rebbe, he's probably an anti-Semite. Who needs it? Better I should go back to Minneapolis where a *mentsh* is a *mentsh* and they have 10,000 lakes instead of 10,000 visitors each day to your house—most don't even wipe their shoes when they come in."

In the end, of course, Grandma Meyer didn't leave, but it took three emergency sessions of the cabinet to negotiate with her before she would settle back to the routine of White House life. A VCR to record her soaps, as well as a non-Jewish attendant who could work it, helped to soften her anger, and, of course, a White House annex was installed over the Golden Age Club in Arlington, Virginia. Finally, she told Jacob: "Okay, for the time being, I'll stay. But I'm warning you. You should be a good boy because the next time I go, I go. You shouldn't take me for granite."

Jacob Meyer served two hectic terms with genuine distinction. Except for the controversiality of Bobby, there was little criticism directed at him or his policies. Most everybody was afraid to express criticism for fear of being accused of anti-Semitism. And, since every citizen served on a subcommittee, the whole nation was part of the Meyer administration. The U.S. was not merely a pure democracy; it was, like Israel, a nation of presidents. Meyer's administration broke the crust of old traditions and old prejudices. He left office on such a swelling wave of democratic sentiment that he was able, miraculously, to handpick his successor and to have her elected against incredible odds: the first black woman ever to serve as president of the United States.

10

Israel: Can It Survive the Peace?

The Arab world has tried every which way to undo the State of Israel: war, attrition, Scuds, terrorism, boycott, using the United Nations as a blunt instrument. But, as the whole world now realizes, *es vet gornisht helfen.* Nothing works. At the end of the day, Israel is still there, an invincible sliver on the map, feisty and enduring.

The Arabs are on the wrong track. There is only one way to defeat the Jewish state. Give the Jews what they most desperately want: peace. Nothing in the world would so destroy the common purpose as removing the common enemy. What would be the Jewish agenda? What would such a catastrophe do to Jewish fund-raising? To rabbinic sermons? To the relationship between Israel and the Diaspora? To Zionism? To Jewish literature? Don't ask. Just imagine the day peace breaks out between Israel and all her neighbors, including the Palestinians. Imagine the moment:

The cabinet meets in special session in Jerusalem. The chief rabbi leads everyone in the *Shehecheyanu* blessing. The prime minister says *L'chayim* in an emotional toast to *shalom.* Arik Sharon denounces the prime minister and warns the cabinet of imminent disaster. The Nachal band plays "*Hatikvah*" and the Saudi national anthem. (The bandleader complained because they worked so hard to learn the Saudi anthem and got to play it only once. And God knows if peace will last long enough for an encore.) The meeting begins.

CABINET MEMBER: Mr. Prime Minister, you must be very proud and happy to have brought peace to Israel after all these years.

P.M.: Proud, yes; happy, no. You all remember what happened to Winston Churchill after he brought England through World War II. Bang, his ungrateful people dumped him out of office and elected a nobody named Clement Attlee.

ANOTHER CABINET MEMBER: It's true. People have short memories. What have you done for me lately? But such a thing could not happen here in Israel. People have such respect for their political leaders. My question is: We survived all those wars and trouble, but can we survive the peace?

CABINET MEMBER: *Bite your tongue.* What did we pray for all these years if not peace?

P.M.: You have a point. But now, without a national emergency, which God had always provided, how do we keep the labor unions from sending inflation off the scope, the religious bloc from amending the Law of Return, the Sephardim from picketing the Soviet Jews, the kibbutzim from . . . ?

MEMBER: Yes. But, bear in mind, peace will surely stimulate tourism!

P.M.: What peace? War turns Jews on. Jews like to visit battlefields, the places where Scuds hit, the Patriots, the generals, the secret airfields. Now, with peace, they are running to Baghdad to see Abraham's birthplace; they are buying *chotchkes* in Damascus and climbing the pyramids in Egypt. And Prince Bandar is the hottest item on the Jewish lecture circuit. . . .

MINISTER FOR ECONOMIC AFFAIRS: I have a bigger worry. Do you see what is happening to the UJA? How do you get Jews to give in peacetime? If we can't scare them, how do we hold them? What slogans will work now? In New York they tried We Shall Overcome and Give Peace a Chance, and they couldn't even get their money back on a full-page ad. What is so yoffee-toffee about peace?

DEFENSE MINISTER: Worse, the Knesset suddenly does not want to spend money on defense. The soldiers don't want to stand guard. They want to play soccer with the Egyptians. And the U.S. Congress is, of course, talking about reducing aid to us. Who needs it?

FOREIGN MINISTER: Look, peace is welcome. Stop *kvetch*ing! This was not an easy achievement on my part, with Baker always breaking my arms and Bush always drawing lines in the sand. Sometimes we Jews have to learn to take *yes* for an answer.

MINISTER IN CHARGE OF ISRAEL-DIASPORA RE-LATIONS: Look, mine is the mother of all *tsores.* What will now keep our people Jewish? Until now, Israel kept them Jewish. Israel was their kidney machine. Fear in the *kishkes* kept them Jewish. Now, if Russia lets out all its Jews, and the peace here holds up, what will keep Jews in America Jewish? Lox and bagels? What will they talk about? God? History? The caterer? There is not even enough anti-Semitism to keep them on their toes.

SECRETARY TO CABINET: But, Mr. Prime Minister, if peace is so dangerous, why did we agree to the terms of the peace treaty?

P.M.: That Baker came to me talking *mama loshen* and said, "Look, just say yes in principle, and leave it to the Arabs in the end to reject. Don't let yourself be blamed for aborting the process. Turns out he said exactly the same thing to the Arabs: Let the Israelis be blamed. So we said yes, and they said yes, and, before either one of us knew what hit us, we were sitting at Camp David signing a peace treaty with a broken hand.

SECRETARY: Thus is history made.

P.M.: Enough *gevald*ism already. It is a *shande* to be terri-fied by peace. Pass me a glass tea. Look, we survived over forty years of war. With a little *mazel,* we can survive peace as well.

SECRETARY: Mr. Prime Minister, the glass tea—you want it half-full or half-empty?

Visit Already, Talk Hebrew

Most visitors see Israel on a frantic two-week tour, much of which is spent whizzing about with one's fellow Americans on a tour bus, dozing in exhaustion, while ancient ruins race by. The tour hurtles you from the Hilton Tel Aviv, to the King David Hotel, to the Dan Carmel in Haifa, to the Galilee, to the Dead Sea, and to Eilat. All the while, a guide drones on about military monuments, and you and your fellow tourists sink into enervated stupors. Unfortunately, traveling in this way, you may never see the inside of a city bus, chat with an Israeli soldier, catch a movie, meet an Arab falafel vendor, or rap with local children in a Jerusalem park.

And there is no better place to achieve Hebrew literacy than your nearest ulpan. Before going to Israel, sign up for one of these intensive language programs. If you are an overachiever, you will no doubt select the six-days-a-week, four-hours-a-day, four-months course. The less ambitious attend three days a week, four hours a day, three months.

Going into ulpan is like going into analysis: It's good for the soul, excellent salon conversation, but, in my case at least, it doesn't work. Like analysis, ulpan is addictive; after you finish, you start again. It can become a way of life, and still you'll talk pidgin Hebrew. Why? Because the language is like an Abbot and Costello routine: In Hebrew, "who" means "he," "he" means "she," "me" means "who," and "dog" means "fish." Hours are feminine, but minutes are masculine. And, if that isn't enough to drive you bats, it reads from right to left.

Ulpan Hebrew bears little resemblance to the language Israelis really speak. In the ulpan, one memorizes charming little conversations for use in a bus, restaurant, barbershop, store, laundry, or theater. Each little scenario is pounded into your head. You burnish it in your mind, polish it, perfect it until the great day comes when you arrive in Israel and try it out on a native—like Jane talking to Tarzan.

"Selichah" (excuse me), you bravely say to the storekeeper, *"ani rotzeh . . ."* (I want . . .)

"English! Talk English!" he orders. "I want to improve my English." (Your store conversation collapses like a house of cards.)

It takes courage to persist if you want to practice your Hebrew on them because they want to practice their English on you. Moreover, one little twist of the tongue can be disastrous. A dear friend of mine, showing off the embryonic ulpan Hebrew he had learned in Cleveland, ordered coffee at a Haifa cafe and, beaming proudly, added *"beli kelev."* It was a small mistake. *Kelev* means "dog"; he meant *chalav,* "cream." Speakers of ulpanese have been known to ask such questions as:

"Do you have a bathroom in your arm?"

"May I buy your sister?"

"Can I sprinkle a king on your meat?"

"Is there a restaurant in the tree?"

Learning Hebrew is partly a function of your polysyllabic skills, if any, the grooves in your brain, and your age. Older people are not so groovy because their brains are downsized. Their children catch the language as if it were a common cold. The result is a peculiar role reversal. When we children of immigrants to America were young, our parents used to speak Yiddish to keep us in the dark. In Israel, the children of American *olim* (immigrants) chatter away comfortably in Hebrew while their greenhorn parents try to sort out "who" is "he" and "he" is "she."

These tongue-tied parents sublimate their frustrations very

effectively in Israel. Women beat their rugs on the balcony, and the men drive their cars like kamikazes, flashing obscene hand signals at every turn.

Thousands of Western immigrants to Israel are breaking their teeth on Hebrew years and years after their arrival. "Hey, I've made it. In America I was always regarded as a Jew. Here I'm regarded as an Anglo-Saxon!"

Some immigrants finally give up the ghost and speak only to their *landsleit*. Others keep trying. One immigrant, a fifteen-year-ulpan veteran, apologized: "I speak only in the present tense, masculine; go shoot me!"

"Show and Tell" is big in ulpan circles. The teacher asks you to describe what you did yesterday. ("I woke up. I ate breakfast. I walked on the street.") Then, the class learns a *sicha* (conversation) about going to a restaurant, a post office, a kitchen. (Some students are excellent in the barbershop, okay in the restaurant, but lousy in the bedroom.)

One American completed his ulpan course in New York City, preparatory to his "trip" to Israel. The teacher gave him a final conversation.

"Atah medaber Ivrit achshav?" (Do you speak Hebrew now?)

"Oui," he replied.

"But that's French."

"Oh," he exulted, "I learned French, too?"

A Quiz

A. True or False

   1. An Israeli WASP is a White Ashkenazic Sabra with Protexia (connections).

   2. Pita is a Jewish puberty rite.

   3. A hora is a reformed prostitute.

4. The leading Japanese convert to Judaism in Israel is an exiled Jewish princess, *Taka Metsiah.*

5. The Law of Return is a law that allows the return of all merchandise from Hamashbir without having to get back on line.

6. *Yekkes* got their name from wearing jackets in the Levantine sun when they first arrived in Israel.

7. The fifth question at the Passover seder is: How come the pages of the *haggadah* keep falling out?

8. The Jewish Eleventh Commandment is: Don't *fonfer!*

B. Multiple Choice
  1. *Hatikvah*   a) A Jewish chastity belt
              b) A herniated ulcer
              c) Mixing kasha and borscht
              d) The Israeli national anthem

  2. *Aliyah*   a) Chief of forty-seven thieves
              b) Fat chef at Camp Kadimah
              c) Aramaic for "Go fall on your head!"
              d) Going to live in Israel

  3. *Kallah*   a) A Jewish bride
              b) A twisted bread
              c) "Color" in Brooklyn
              d) A religious conference, winding up with the question: Where do we go from here?
              e) Arabic for my *killah* is your *gedillah*

  4. *Kine Ahora* a) A black eye
              b) Your kin dancing the hora
              c) A Jewish male doll
              d) Jewish response to good news

5. *Nosh*ing
   a) A sacred rite
   b) Hebrew for "nothing"
   c) Bonding between Reform and Ortho-dox Jews
   d) *Chutzpah,* which is graceful gall, co-opted by Dershowitz
   e) Eat, eat, my child

6. *Fonfer*ing
   a) An Oriental Jewish food
   b) Bonding between Ashkenazic and Sephardic Jews
   c) Jewish skywriting
   d) Jewish stammering

7. Chasidim
   a) A Jewish Orthodox sect
   b) Jewish *dim sum*
   c) A Hebrew-speaking mugger, crying gimme loot, *chasadim*!
   d) An Arab village in the Galilee
   e) Hebrew for the crazy way Israelis drive

8. Sharon
   a) An Israeli whoopie cushion
   b) A fat Israeli general
   c) A Jewish gazelle that runs from right to left
   d) A Jewish falafel
   e) The Nancy Reagan of Israel
   f) A Tel Aviv waiter who demands, "Okay, who ordered the clean glass?"

If you wish to know the correct answers, so do I.

11

Jewish Names:
How Kimberly and Chad
Begat Adam and Tamar

At a recent United Jewish Appeal seminar in the Midwest, three generations of American Jews were represented. The "Hello, I am . . ." tags revealed interesting genealogical differences. The middle-aged and older "boys" sported stolid first names such as Marvin, Melvin, Milton, Morris, and Max (with a few Howards, Alberts, and Irvings); and "the girls" included Thelma, Helen, Sadie, Edith, Ruth, and Gladys.

Their children brandished such chic American monickers as Rex, Blake, Scott, Chad, and Brad; their female counterparts: Kimberly, Bambi, Kathi, Wendi, Margo, Dawn, and Cindy.

This young Americanized generation—products of the decade of the youth culture and the most traumatic era of recent American history—has produced smaller families (average: two children, alarmingly closer to the goal of zero population growth than any other group in American life), but they have—generally and unaccountably—stamped many more Jewish brands on their progeny. Among *their* children, the most popular names seem to be Aaron, Abraham, Adam, Seth, and David, or Rachel, Zachary, Rebecca, Tamar, Naomi, Aviva, Zipporah, and Jonah.

What's going on here? How come? American Jewish names are proving the validity of the sociologists' classic maxim about ethnic groups: The grandchildren want to remember what their parents wanted to forget. But, wait! That batch of Jewish toddlers didn't name themselves. How did it happen that Kimberly and Chad begat Adam and Tamar?

The dizzying changes in first names reflect profound cultural and ethnic changes in American life. Only two generations ago, Jews—like other immigrant groups—were hellbent on diving headfirst into the American melting pot where, in accordance with conventional mythology, they would emerge as Americans in gray flannel suits. Shaken by anti-Semitism and anti-Jewish discrimination, many Jews were quick to change their noses and their family names in order to "pass" in a deracinated WASP America.

All that has changed dramatically. The vaunted melting pot never really worked. Instead of melting, each group lay in the pot, simmering in separate globs. It wasn't a melting pot; it was a stew, a smorgasbord—and indigestible. The American way is to make a virtue out of necessity, so America hailed the failure of the melting pot and called it religious and cultural pluralism. The false image of the melting pot was replaced by the romantic image of an orchestra, combining the distinctive tones and ambience of a dozen separate instruments into one magnificent symphony. Did we Jews clang the cymbals or beat the drums? What difference? We were assuredly one of the kids in the band—accepted and respected—and we helped America to play sweet music. Sometimes we went beyond pluralism and conceptualized a three-faith America in which we Jews (3 percent of the population) emerged on center stage as one of three equal faiths (33 ⅓ percent)—a stunning public relations coup.

Indeed, millions of young Americans, including many Jews, have gone back to their roots. Israel has had a magnetic impact on Jewish self-awareness. Courses in Jewish studies have bloomed on a thousand campuses. Jewish religious and cultural camps have filled to overflowing while private (color-war) camps have languished. YIVO, in New York City, which three decades ago threatened to become a Jewish mausoleum, has found itself thronged with young Jews fervently mastering the Yiddish language and exploring their grandparents' origins in Warsaw and Posen and Zhitomir.

In biblical times, names conveyed certain characteristics or experiences. The name "Isaac" flows from the Hebrew word for "laughter" because Sarah, wife of Abraham, burst into laughter when she learned she would bear a son at the unlikely age of ninety. The variety of names is evident in that one finds very few repeats in the long list of "begats" in the Bible—our forefathers looked upon each child as unique. During most of Jewish history, we did not have surnames. Surnames appeared among Sephardic Jews in the Middle Ages and among Ashkenazic Jews probably in the eighteenth century. In 1787, the Austrian government issued a decree that required Jews to adopt surnames.

Not so many generations ago, when we acquired family names, there was often nothing Jewish about them. Our forefathers often borrowed vocational names: A shoemaker became Schuster; a printer became Drucker; a tailor, Schneider; a merchant, Kaufman; a miller, Miller; a gardener, Gartner. We are not certain whether a painter became Paintner, but Sam Schmuckler did not, as might be suspected, bribe an official to add the last three letters.

Many Jews got their names from the map. Such family names as Berlin, Warsaw, Danzig, Halpern, Posner (from the city of Posen), Brody, Horowitz, and Ginsberg sprang right from the accidents of geography. In other cases, anti-Jewish officials afflicted their Jewish subjects with such names as Eselkopf (donkey's head) and Fresser (glutton). Thus, most of the names we now think of as very Jewish have non-Jewish origins. Names ending in "vich" are Russian, "sohn" is German, and "ski" is Polish. So what's Jewish about Jewish family names? Cohen, Levy, and Israel may be the only completely Jewish surnames in use.

Jews once tried to flee their Jewishness, sometimes changing their noses, names, and life-styles in order to melt into a WASPish America. No more. Now we know the melting pot doesn't melt—it's more like a juicy *bouillabaisse,* and ethnic differences are vital and here to stay. Look at the many Jewish names currently in the U.S. Senate: Levin, Metzenbaum, Wellstone, Lieberman, Lautenberg, Specter, Kohl, and Rudman.

A Jewish name is no longer a political liability; it may even be a plus. Even non-Jews like Senator Bill Cohen of Maine don't bother to change their Jewish names. Why should they? They may get money unwittingly from Jewish PACs, especially if they have the good fortune of being zinged by anti-Semites. A 1990 senatorial race in Minnesota between Wellstone and Boschwitz actually revolved around a question of Who is the better Jew! Indeed an Israeli newspaper headlined this Minnesota brouhaha: The "Bad Jew" Beats the "Good Jew," Thank God. So a Jewish name may be a polysyllabic jawbreaker, but it has more political mileage than a neuter Anglo-Saxon moniker.

A new wrinkle in names—Jewish and non-Jewish—is the current trend toward two last names. Reflecting the lure of feminism, many couples now travel under the combined names of the wife and husband. I know one American Jewish woman named Aliya. Her parents, both active Zionists, were frustrated about their inability to move to Israel and thus named their daughter Aliya so they could feel, correctly, that they "finally made *aliyah.*" Aliya married a man named Cotel (pronounced the same as Jerusalem's Western Wall). She now calls herself Aliya Cheskis-Cotel, a fine Jewish mouthful.

I know a Jewish man named Aron, a writer, whose surname was Manheimer (deriving from a German city). He married

Judith Hirt. Tracing her family background, they found that the name Hirt ("shepherd" in German) goes all the way back to the Abravanel family of Spain. Because Judith had no brother, and she and her husband felt strongly that her family name should be maintained, the young couple legally changed their names to Aron and Judith Hirt-Manheimer, thus paying homage in one fell swoop to Jewish ancestral traditions, feminism, and Jewish survivalism. Their first child is named Noah, the second Isaac, and the third is Miriam Tsipporah Hirt-Manheimer. So what else is new?

God knows what will happen if my fifth grandchild, Jonah Sidney Vorspan-Stein, should fall in love someday with a young lady named Rebecca Lila Rosenkranz-Fergassen!

12

The Kishkes Factor

Jews are widely and correctly regarded as well educated, bright overachievers—as smart as ten colleges. Among culture *maven*s they rank high. They are both producers and consumers of art, literature, and music. Without Jews the Great White Way would be dark; Broadway theaters would be empty; publishers would die on the vine. But what is less understood is that Jews think not only with their heads. They think with their *kishkes*—roughly translated, their gut. Behold, the *kishkes* factor!

Take anti-Semitism for an example. There are careful studies that demonstrate that anti-Semitism in America has declined sharply since World War II. Indeed, the presence in 1991 of *eight* Jews in the U.S. Senate—some coming from such non-Jewish states as Minnesota, Ohio, Michigan—seems to confirm the scientific evidence that discrimination against Jews is now minimal and that anti-Jewish prejudice has dribbled to a low ebb after the heydays of Father Coughlin and the Ku Klux Klan. That's what the polls and studies show, even studies done by the American Jewish Committee. But, of course, that's not what ordinary Jews believe. They believe their *kishkes*. And their *kishkes* say *gevald*—roughly translated, when things look good, beware!

Why listen to their *kishkes* instead of to the smarty-pants? Jewish *kishkes* have been tutored by a unique, sublime, and tormented history. Every Jew has a *kishke* trained by three thousand years of persecution. The *kishke* functions like radar, identifying friend and foe at any distance. While the ineffable Kurt Waldheim was presiding over the United Nations like a striped-pants demigod, Jewish *kishkes* were already emitting silent signals that he was a no-goodnik; hard evidence of Waldheim's Nazi background didn't emerge until years later.

When the demagogue Joe McCarthy was polluting the U.S. Senate and the country with his poison gas—even though he sought a kosher label by surrounding himself with two Jewish itinerant punks (Cohn and Schine)—Jews saw through him faster than any segment of the American population. Why? Their *kishkes* were vibrating like burglar alarms. In the *kishke,* historic memories of Haman, Torquemada, and Antiochus—tyrants and hate-mongers who have littered Jewish history—are mingled into one sour mash. More recently, Jews smelled that Saddam Hussein was bad news before he was Saddamized by George Bush. In their *kishkes,* Jews drew a bead on this malevolent character, placing him in the context of history, asking what else is new? How delicious that Saddam's defeat came on the evening of Purim, the holiday commemorating the fall of Haman!

The Jewish *kishke* is tellingly accurate. When Vice-President Agnew turned his venomous tongue to a campaign against intellectuals, liberals, and the media, he never mentioned Jews. So wouldn't it be paranoid to associate him with anti-Semitism? Jewish *kishkes* blew silent whistles. Much later, after all the air went out of his balloon and he was just another loud-mouthed felon, his antipathy to Jews and Israel oozed out publicly. But Jewish *kishkes* had skewered him as a crook and a bigot while he was still masquerading as a public servant and giving felons a bad name.

But our Jewish *kishkes* are not infallible. There have been fascinating studies in which non-Jews were tested on their attitudes toward Jews. Then Jews were tested on what *they* thought the non-Jews thought. The non-Jews generally reflected some anti-Jewish stereotyping but not too much and decidedly less than ever before. (Anti-Semitism has been defined by cynics as disliking Jews more than absolutely necessary.) But the Jews in our test assumed that the non-Jews thought the worst. *Voilà,* the *kishke* factor!

What can you expect from a *kishke* after three millennia of tender ministrations at the hands of Christians, Muslims, and nonbelievers? Jewish *kishkes* are no doubt laced with a touch of paranoia, but just because you are paranoid doesn't mean you don't have real enemies.

Jewish *kishkes* work overtime on Israel. Since anti-Semitism nowadays often parades as anti-Zionism ("I have nothing against Jews and Judaism, but Israel sucks."), Jewish *kishkes* sometimes overreact to non-Jewish criticism of Israel. *Jewish* criticism of Israel, on the other hand, is par for the course, especially for Israelis, and American Jews even enjoy some cachet for dissent from hard-line Israeli policies. Let a non-Jew tell the same JAP joke, and the Jewish *kishke* lets out a *gevald.* Go figure!

Now it's time to test your *kishkes* as you review the names below. If your *kishke* is unaffected, score 0. If your *kishke* twitches lightly, 1. If the *kishke* writhes like you had too much hot pastrami, 2. If the *kishke* turns over like your car motor on a subzero day, 3. If your entire stomach rumbles as though you were about to face root canal work and/or a pogrom, 4. If the *kishke* lights up and tilts the machine, 5! Put the number next to each name, and then add. If the total is higher than 20, you are Jewish to the max, whether you know it or not. (Perhaps you got it intravenously.)

	SCORE
Richard Nixon	＿＿＿
Peter Jennings	＿＿＿
Robert Novak	＿＿＿
Gore Vidal	＿＿＿
Peter Arnett	＿＿＿

SCORE

Hafez al-Assad   ———

Lyndon LaRouche   ———

Yassir Arafat   ———

Pat Robertson   ———

Jerry Falwell   ———

Jesse Jackson   ———

Mikhail Gorbachev   ———

Louis Farrakhan   ———

Sen. Robert Dole   ———

David Duke   ———

Jesse Helms   ———

Pat Buchanan   ———

13

Shlepping for God: Travails of a Traveling Organization Man

As a member of the staff of a large national Jewish organization, it is my fate to do a substantial bit of traveling. I seemed to find myself en route to or from some distant place much more often than could be easily explained to a patient wife and an impatient brood of children. Fastening my seat belt and waving guiltily in the direction of my glaring family, I would comfort myself with the assurance that my sacrifice was good for the Jews, that, in a sense, I was *shlepp*ing for God. (But interposed my nagging conscience: your family—they're not Jews, too?) Travel also is broadening and earns lots of frequent flyer miles so one can travel even more.

Many years ago, I was sent to Atlantic City to handle publicity for an organization's convention. Hoping to enjoy a brief stay at the seashore, I brought my wife with me. It was made clear to me by the officials that the opportunities for good publicity at this convention were *shvach* (a Jewish word that means you should live so long). Specifically, I was told that the only real newspaper story I had was that the convention would be addressed by the recently elected and exceedingly dynamic Senator Hubert Humphrey of Minnesota. But even this was no bonanza because, I was told, the senator had not produced an advance manuscript, would be speaking off the cuff, and my only chance for a press release was to nail him privately beforehand. The senator had notified the convention officials that he would arrive by train the afternoon of his evening address. My instructions were to grab him at the station and pump him for a quote.

My wife and I cased the depot. She stationed herself on one end of the platform and I on the other. Neither of us could remember what the senator looked like. As the train puffed into the station, total confusion ensued. Vacation-bound men and women poured off the cars and disappeared into the line of taxicabs pulled up along the platform. With mounting panic, I ran from man to man, peering into each face. My wife was disporting herself with similar frenzy at the other end of the platform. Suddenly, I heard a welcome word. Somebody was yelling, "Senator! Senator!" Sighing with relief, I looked up and, sure enough, there stood a handsome, vigorous man, briefcase in hand. He struck a pose of unquestioned authority and distinction.

I raced up to him, extending my hand, and announced: "Good afternoon, Senator, my name is Vorspan, I'm here to . . ."

Inexplicably, he didn't take my hand. He gazed at me with a look of fear and confusion. He must not have heard me.

"Senator! Senator!" the cry went up again. It must be Senator Humphrey, I reasoned, knowing that, if he should escape me, abysmal failure would be certain. I had to make him understand.

"Look, Senator, please. I'm the publicity man for this convention. I'm here to talk to you about your speech; we need some quotes for the press. . . ."

The curious look in his eye became wild. I put my hand gently on his arm. He pulled it away with revulsion. He began to run. I pursued him. My wife, sensing disaster, joined the chase. Running full stride, he jumped into a waiting taxi, slammed the door tight, pressed down the lock button, and, shaking his head, stared out at me as he escaped.

My wife and I exchanged defeated looks. We had let our quarry escape. Just then the cab driver poked his head out the window and bellowed: "This cab for the Senator! Anybody else for the Senator Hotel!"

I looked at my shoes. My wife looked at her shoes. Finally, she spoke: "What kind of business is publicity for a nice Jewish boy anyway?"

I don't always have to travel far to find trouble. My trip to White Plains, New York, a couple of years back still haunts me.

A colleague in my office pleaded with me to pinch-hit for him as a speaker. "Nothing to it," he assured me. "An interfaith group of ladies. They have this annual thing. It's a panel discussion, you know, a Protestant, a Catholic, and a Jew. Well, you're the Jew. Each member of the panel will talk for about ten minutes, no more, something on 'Religion and the World Peace.' The usual thing."

Thus briefed, I drove along the sunlit parkways, working out a short, informal talk in my mind. The meeting was at a large Episcopal church. The chairwoman met me at the door, where an interfaith service was going on, and conducted me into the dining room where, she said, she wanted to introduce me to some people. To my mild surprise, the dining room was arranged for quite a large assembly. Gathered at the head table were several local dignitaries, including an impressive number of clergymen of all faiths.

The first premonitory anxiety hit me. "By the way," I said to the chairwoman casually, "don't you think I should spend a minute or two with the other panelists before we go on?"

Her expression went blank. "The what?"

"You know," I said, "the Protestant and the Catholic panelists; we ought to work out the details . . . who goes first . . . things like that. . . ."

After a long pause, the lady said: "Mr Vorspan, this dining room will soon be filled with about 250 ladies. They have, all of them, paid for this luncheon and have come here, in good faith, to hear an address. I repeat: 'an address.' Our entire program is one major address on the subject 'Religion and the United Nations.' The speaker is Mr. Albert Vorspan. That is you, is it not?"

I sometimes wonder if what I said that afternoon in White Plains had anything to do with the UN's subsequent descent into anti-Zionism and obscurity.

Once, when our four children were young, my wife and I threw the brood into the Chevy and drove from New York to Miami in the winter to catch some sun and take advantage of my speaking tour in Florida. We visited family, swam, and enjoyed the sun. Finally it was time for my wife and the kids to drive back to New York and for me to get to work on a series of speeches. Shirley and our kids drove me to the Howard Johnson in Palm Beach. I got out of the car, kissed everybody, grabbed my matched suitcase (I thought), and raced into the hotel in my bermuda shorts and T-shirt with only one hour to prepare my notes. The family scooted off to I95.

Upstairs, I opened my suitcase to unpack. *Oy, vey!* It was my daughter Deborah's matched suitcase, not mine! It contained—altogether—four boxes of tampax, three pairs of women's undies, a bra, a toothbrush, and a large hairdrier!

Once when I was booked to speak at a Jewish community center in a large Texas community, the well-respected rabbi of the nearby synagogue asked me to meet informally with him and the staffs of various local Jewish agencies the afternoon before my speech. After the rabbi introduced me most handsomely to the thirty or so pros who had gathered on short notice, he sat down right next to me. I stood up, expressed my pleasure at this invitation, and turned to thank the rabbi for his warm introduction. Presto, he was already in deep and resonant slumber and stayed that way until I finished my remarks. At that point he rose, refreshed, put his hand on my shoulder affectionately, and said: "Al, I've heard you speak dozens of times, but I never enjoyed you more than today."

Perhaps my most unforgettable experience as a speaker was when I returned decades later to the Twin Cities, my birthplace, to be introduced by somebody I had never met while growing up with God's frozen people. The introducer, disclaiming the canned bio sent along in advance, did original research into my early life. By interviewing my beloved Aunt Sophie, then eighty-six, he learned the vagaries of my childhood, including my checkered career as a newspaper delivery boy and part-time juvenile delinquent. Finally, the soaring peroration: "My friends, I take great pride in presenting to you tonight this son of . . . the Twin Cities, who has made contributions to Jewish life—indeed to America—nay, to all humanity—that can only be described as—*infinitesimal*."

Several of my colleagues and I had somehow tapped into the bonanza of serving on the faculty of an elegant Jewish adult-education cruise to Alaska. What a gig! As the comfortable S.S. Sagafjord navigated the breathtaking fjords and ice-blue glaciers on the exquisitely beautiful cruise from Vancouver to Anchorage, my colleagues and I divided up the lectures that were to be presented in the ship's theater on days when the passengers did not go ashore to visit such romantic ports of call as Sitka and Homer. Believe it or not, we were met at the dock by singing Jewish youths, wearing Hebrew T-shirts saying *Ani Ohev Alaska* ("I love Alaska").

The highlight of the cruise was the captain's party, an afternoon bash in which everybody went topside to fill up on the Scandanavian Aquavit liquor and lobsters. The orgy of food and drinks, under a brilliant sun, while the ship passed scenes of indescribable grandeur, intoxicated the passengers. Unfortunately, I was scheduled to lecture in the theater at 3:00 P.M.

on "Jewish Humor." The ship was heaving slightly, and so were some of the passengers. Within minutes, the theater looked like a war zone. Open-mouthed bodies hung from every seat. Snores rattled from porthole to porthole. An old lady dropped from her seat and rolled gently down the aisle, apologizing sweetly to me for the interruption. The rabbi who was supposed to introduce me hit the deck with a thud, murmuring: "Serves me right for eating *trayf*" and then he went out like a light unto the nations. Me, I didn't need an introduction. I needed a conclusion.

My good friend and coworker Rabbi Eugene Lipman and I had just coauthored a book entitled *A Tale of Ten Cities,* a study of interfaith relations in America, which our publicity man hyped as five times bigger than Dickens. We did the usual book tour, which, in the case of our book, usually consisted of Ruth Jacobs on radio station WEVD in New York City and TV programs in the early-dawn religious ghetto timeslot on Sundays. However, we wangled a prime-time radio talk show interview in Omaha, with a non-Jewish interviewer whose familiarity with things Jewish was foggy at best. He began to question us about the internal Jewish scene—relations among Orthodox, Conservative, and Reform Jews. Gene explained that we all believe in the imperative of the *mitzvah* (commandment to do good) but interpret it differently.

"Wait," asked the interviewer, "what is this about kosher slaughtering, and how is it done?" I plunged in with a complicated answer and heard myself saying, "It has to do with the ritual slaughter of Orthodox Jews." Whoops! I had just recovered, gracelessly, when Gene launched into such examples of the Jewish *mitzvah* as visiting the dead and burying the sick. Our book sold out in Omaha—all four copies—and two authors limped on to Chicago suffering a bad case of foot-in-mouth disease.

Early in my career, there were occasions when it was necessary to share a room with another member of the staff. However, after one such experience in Washington, D.C., I drew the line in the sand and proclaimed never again. My staff roommate on that occasion was one of my best friends, a savvy political *maven* and a world-class guy. How was I to know that he snored, that his snoring roared like the helicopter landing in the middle of *Miss Saigon,* and that noise filtering through his fulsome beard would bounce through the hotel room from wall to wall. For the first hour, I tried to read. The snore reverberated through my head. I turned on "The Tonight Show," real loud, determined to drown out my friend. Could it be that he was also turning up his own volume? After two hours, I began to panic. I was exhausted, my eyes were closed, but I couldn't sleep. In desperation, I got out of bed, pleading with a catatonic Pete to lower his volume. Nothing. I shook his shoulder. Nothing. I found some cotton, stuffed my ears, and pulled the covers over my head. Nothing. I pulled the covers over his beard. The helicopter was still flying over Saigon, my head was pounding, and I knew the moment of truth had arrived. I either had to terminate my roommate or my agony.

I took all my bedding, marched into the bathroom, closed the door tightly to screen out the din, and settled myself into the bathtub. Alas, the bathtub had a small leak—dripping cold water on my blanket. Despite everything, my exhaustion finally prevailed, and I fell into a deep sleep. Then, in the dim outline of dawn's early light, I perceived a large hulking and bearded form, scratching and still snoring sonorously, approaching the toilet. In the midst of his ablutions, he seemed to become vaguely aware of a foreign presence in the room— me. Without the slightest loss of volume, he turned slowly, blankly, blinking slightly, and peered down at me, twisted in the damp bathtub. "What the hell are you doing in there?" he asked.

"Everybody's got to be somewhere," I explained.

"Oh," he replied.

Never, in all the subsequent years we worked together, did my bearded colleague ever refer to that cacophonous night. I have never again had occasion to sleep in a bathtub, and I have always found an excuse not to share a hotel room, a camp cabin, or even a stateroom with anybody except my wife.

Once upon a time a presidential candidate pulled out of the race, complaining that he had slept in one too many Holiday Inns. Okay, but what's the alternative? A quaint, charming, historic little hotel, once frequented by William Penn, deep in Pennsylvania's picturesque Bucks County, set on a lovely block of touristy antique shops dating back to 1720. Right? Wrong.

After a long drive from New York, replete with bottlenecks and detours, I arrive on Friday afternoon in plenty of time for Shabbat dinner with the rabbi and my speech at the synagogue service. Making my way to the hotel, which is located on the narrow main street of this tiny old town, I find a parking spot at the curb and go to the hotel to check in.

"Where can I park my car?" I ask. "Do you have a parking lot? I'll be here for the weekend."

"No," she smiles, "but you can leave it on the street."

"Oh, fine. Is that legal?"

"No. You have to move it every two hours."

Finally, I find a clandestine parking spot in an alley behind a church and go back to my hotel to get my room. The hotel is too quaint for elevators—or room numbers. It is a maze of bare, wide-planked floors with ten old-fashioned rooms, all named after historic personalities. I am assigned to General Stewart, which is on the third floor, reachable only by an unlighted and narrow staircase. "Oh, by the way," the clerk says after escorting me through the labyrinthine passageways, "your telephone is a bit messed up. Just dial 9, then hang up, then dial 9 again."

I try to call the desk to ask if there is room service. There isn't, it turns out, but you can't call the desk either—not on this phone. I spend the rest of the afternoon trying to call my wife. First 9, then hang up, then 9 again. No use. Finally, I walk down to the desk and use the switchboard to call home to tell my wife everything is fine. Finding General Stewart again in the rabbit's warren is a struggle—it is left of Fabian and across from the Ohillian Higgs Stagecoach stop. I finally make it and decide to sit down to work on my speech. But, alas, the only lamp is decidedly quaint and charming—but the bulb is burned out. I can't call down to the desk, and I'll be damned if I will risk going down and getting lost once more somewhere between the restaurant and the tavern, or between Violetta's Chamber and William's Cupboard.

Next time, if there is a next time—because for me the Bucks stops here—they can please book me into a boring, predictable Holiday Inn, with a swimming pool, parking lot, room service, bellhop, cable TV, elevator, and a plastic lamp that works. Too much quaint leaves me speechless.

Epilogue

Did you enjoy this book? If not, you really have a lousy sense of humor, and I can do without your opinion.

In any event, this book is my last hurrah while I am still in the saddle of Jewish organizational life. Remembering Woody Allen's insight that 70 percent of success is showing up, I have had a terrific career in my forty years of Jewry duty. This book has helped me to sublimate the retirement blues. It may not have done all that much for you, but for me it was superb. Without a capacity for laughter, life is tough. I'm reminded of the classic story about the Jewish woman who was learning about the laughing hyena at the zoo. The guide explained that the hyena has sex only twice a year. The lady pondered this information and replied in Yiddish: *Vus kvelt er, de chaya?* "So what's this animal got to laugh about?"

Before I ride away into the sunset, I want to share with you a fascinating experience. (Tell me, when will I get another chance?) In 1990 I was invited, along with seven other representatives of national Jewish agencies, to meet with the Dalai Lama of Tibet. Of course, driving to the retreat center in New Jersey to meet with him, we made all the dumb and predictable jokes: *Hello, Dolly* and *Early Tibet and early to rise,* etc. But the meeting was not funny. It was unforgettable.

The Dalai Lama himself is colorful and engaging. Wearing brown and purple robes, perched comfortably on a couch with his legs crossed under him, a warm smile lighting up his face despite all the grimness of his situation, a puckish sense of humor crinkling his eyes at unexpected moments, the Dalai

Lama greeted us and, in a soft voice, told us of the thirty-year campaign of genocide his Tibetan people had experienced at the hands of the Chinese invaders. We expressed our deep concern at the ongoing destruction of Tibetan religious, ethnic, and national identity. He was grateful, but he had something on his mind other than mutual commiseration. "Tell me," he said, *what is your secret?* How can a people that has been persecuted and exiled and vilified throughout the centuries maintain its religion and its sense of national identity? No other people has done this, except you. I want to know your secret to help preserve my people."

We gave a variety of responses to the Dalai Lama. One told the story of Yochanan ben Zakkai and how his small school at Yavneh preserved the Jewish values, which somehow outlasted the Roman conquest of Judea. Another explained the story of modern Israel itself, of how the Jewish people, exiled for centuries, achieved national liberation out of the ashes of the Holocaust. The miracle of Israel was a product of faith, memory, and peoplehood. Some of us said that the Dalai Lama had already learned our secret in his own championship of the values of nonviolent resistance to evil, the quality for which he was honored by the entire civilized world. The power of the spirit, which he helps to symbolize in the world today, is ultimately more powerful than all the armies and weapons of repression. In that, both his people and our Jewish people share a common vision of peace, justice, and gentle relations among all the brothers and sisters of the world.

One of our group said that persecution keeps a people alive. Thanks a lot (go tell it to the Kurds)! Another said that Judaism, as a way of life, was the key to Jewish survival and that the synagogue is the fount of Jewish immortality. Another said Jewish humor was the force that kept Jews human in times of acute pressure, recalling one Jew's riposte to an anti-Semite: "When your people were still swinging from trees, my people had already discovered the peptic ulcer."

I added that the Jewish passion for social justice had made a difference not only to Jews but to all the world. The refusal to yield to despair, fatigue, or cynicism; the stubborn belief in *tikun olam* (repairing the world); the *chutzpadik* notion that we are copartners with God in refashioning a humane and civilized world—these Jewish compulsions have helped preserve the Jewish spirit.

Do Jews still have a passion for social justice? A young Jewish woman, a social activist in California, put it this way: "Most people in our world live heroic lives merely trying to survive for one more day. They are powerless to evoke change, let alone help others. That is why I feel so strongly that those of us who can make things better must do so. And, if we don't, we are depriving ourselves of perhaps the greatest opportunity life can offer: to help change the world and, in turn, give true meaning to our lives."

One of the nicest traditions in Jewish life is the ethical will. Alas, it has been allowed to fade out of the lives of most modern Jews. What a loss! The ethical will, which our ancestors passed on to their children, did not list material assets and properties. It contained one's most important asset: the accumulated values and wisdom that, at the end of the day, he wished to pass on as his proudest legacy to his survivors. Nowadays, if we could restore this beautiful tradition, it would of course be done by mothers as well as fathers. Just think how satisfying it would be to identify and pass on those imperishable values—not just the rusty 1984 Subaru and the house—that really count and that stand the test of a lifetime. So my ethical will is simple: Life is precious, nurture it; take the world seriously, and strive always to improve it; and respect yourself, but don't take yourself too seriously, lest you find yourself (in words I stole from Shakespeare) "blown up by your own wind."

So what will happen at the end of days? There is a story that the apocalypse finally came, and the world's religious leaders convened their congregations. The Christian minister preached about Noah and concluded Judgment Day was at hand. The Muslim pastor preached Allah is great and martyrdom is blessed in the world to come. The Buddhist monk said to hold on to your karma and remember the wheel of life is eternal so what goes around comes around. The Unitarian minister pleaded To Whom It May Concern. And the rabbi organized swimming lessons.

So choose life and live. But, in the meantime, start worrying: details to follow.